D0579327

LEE BAILEY'S
COUNTRY FLOWERS

Other Gardening Books from Random House Value Publishing, Inc.:

American Gardens

Tips for the Lazy Gardener

The Romantic Rose

The Complete Gardener

The Essential Gardener

LEE BAILEY'S COUNTRY FLOWERS

Gardening and Bouquets from Spring to Fall

Text and Photographs by Lee Bailey

GRAMERCY BOOKS
New York

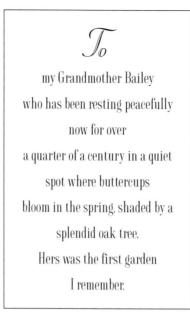

To
my Grandmother Bailey
who has been resting peacefully
now for over
a quarter of a century in a quiet
spot where buttercups
bloom in the spring, shaded by a
splendid oak tree.
Hers was the first garden
I remember.

Copyright © 1985 by Lee Bailey

All rights reserved. No part of this book may be reproduced or transmitted in any form or by any means, electronic or mechanical, including photocopying, recording, or by any information storage and retrieval system, without permission in writing from the publisher.

This 1997 edition is published by Gramercy Books, an imprint of Random House Value Publishing, Inc. by arrangement with Clarkson N. Potter, a member of the Crown Publishing Group.

Designed by Rochelle Udell with Rise Daniels

Gramercy Books and colophon are trademarks of Random House Value Publishing, Inc.

Random House
New York . Toronto . London . Sydney . Auckland
http://www.randomhouse.com/

Printed and bound in China

Library of Congress Cataloging-in-Publication Data

Bailey, Lee.
[Country Flowers]
Lee Bailey's country flowers: gardening and bouquets from spring to fall / text and photographs by Lee Bailey.
p.   cm.
Originally published: New York: C.N. Potter, 1985.
Includes index.
ISBN 0-517-18742-6
1.   Flower gardening. 2.   Flowers.   I. Title.
SB405.B246   1997
635.9'66—dc21   97-12225
CIP

Lee Bailey's Country Flowers
ISBN: 0-517-18742-6

Contents

Acknowledgments

For Carolyn Hart Gavin, my editor, for her usual expert work and support and more—also to all the rest of the marvelous team at Clarkson N. Potter, thanks and gratitude.

For my Bendel's team, Carole Bannett and Joan Muli, for doing everything so well, as usual. And for Tony Diaz.

For Geraldine Stutz, on general principles.

For Rochelle Udell, who never fails me—this time with an assist by Rïse Daniels.

For Gloria Safier, with love.

To Pamela Lord for all that research and enthusiasm and help beyond the call of duty.

And to the brothers Skidmore, Peter and Perry, for making a nice place for me to work.

For Tony Babinski, who good-naturedly grew and gathered wonderful flowers for me—and to his wife, Teresa, a self-confessed "flower-nut."

For Peter Cooper, who supplied additional beautiful flowers and helpful comments. And Debbie Van Bourgondien for her help—same to Chris Becker.

For Agusta Maynard and Ben Baldwin for some absolutely breathtaking roses.

For Carol Mercer, for letting me photograph her perfect perennial border.

To Michael Newhard, for painting some lovely backgrounds. And thanks to Lothian Lynas, of the New York Botanical Gardens, who checked over my amateur identifications and Latin spellings.

To Judy Corman (Judy Corman, Inc.) and Stephanie and Morgan Rank (Rank, Inc.) for letting me use their beautiful old linens and quilts.

For giving me the use of a selection of their glorious crystal, thanks to Tiffany & Co. with the assistance of Joe Pugliese. And to Joe Minton for his collection of Roman glass.

For Dick Camp (Dick Camp, Inc.) and Susan Costner (C & W Mercantile) for things from their wonderful shops.

For Don Zoltow of American Wing Antiques with appreciation for loads of terrific things—and the same to Mrs. Joyce Nicholas, owner of Pine St. Antiques, with an able assist by Shirley Johnson.

To Wendy Engle at Engle Pottery for African bowls and baskets—and practically next door, thanks to Poster Originals. Then down the street at Dean & Deluca, thanks to Dorothy Bates and Claire Callihan.

My appreciation to Pheasant Antiques.

Thanks to my two potter friends, Barbara Eigen and Ann Weber. And for Florence Fink for trying to find ways to make things easier—and for David Luck.

For Liz Smith, with love and friendship. For over twenty years of watching this garden grow with me, and for her occasionally trenchant comments. Like the year I planted a long bed of white petunias, and she told me they looked like a bunch of used tissues in the yard. I hated it that she was right.

Finally, for Joshua Greene, whose beautiful and sensitive photographs for my first two books opened my eyes to things I had been looking at for years. Thanks. And thanks for showing me how to load the camera.

Introduction

A passing remark from my aunt about how I used to trail around after my Grandmother Bailey in the garden conjured up an image from a time I had almost forgotten—of Grannie, a sturdy five feet tall; of Ellis, our yardman, a stratospheric six feet something; and of a stringy little five-year-old boy with white hair (who grew up to be me). She was called "Mamaw," and I was "Cotton Top." Ellis was called "as skinny as a snake" by his wife, Lurlee, our cook. Led by the always bemused (in my recollection) Mamaw, walking Indian file, we toured the yard as she gave orders: "Move that, Ellis."—"Yesum." "Cut those back to the quick."—"Yesum." "You think *all those* weeds are doing the roses any good?"—"Nome." "Honey, how many times do I have to tell you not to stand in the four-o'clocks; red bugs'll eat you alive."—"Yes, ma'am." Occasionally during these campaigns, Ellis would catch my eye out of sight of the general, and a sheepish smile would animate his otherwise expressionless face—to let me know we were really just humoring her. It was better that way. I understood.

Now that my memory has been jogged, I remember these tours vividly and the thrill I felt at being part of the action. At first, I imagine, just being included was enough, but later I started to share my grandmother's enthusiasm for growing things. Back then her passion had been roses and japonicas. Mine was zinnias, larkspur, and poppies—which I like to this day. I suppose she was pleased to have a grandchild who liked what she did, although this was never expressed in words—only in the tacit acceptance of me as part of the team.

The only time I ever got in trouble with her about the garden was over an enormous patch of violets that had overgrown a side bed and came into spectacular bloom in the spring. Actually, it wasn't the violets, but a dog named Queenie. We always kept lots of dogs—beagles, setters, and bird dogs—all hunters. Among them was the imperious Queenie, my father's favorite, who liked nothing better than a nap in the sacred violet bed. Since I loved her just about on a par with the other members of my family, whatever she liked was OK by me, so I loved to lie in the violet bed with her. I can still feel how cool the leaves were on my face, and smell the sweet little purple flowers. Queenie was right, of course. Unfortunately, this relaxed tableau didn't do the flowers much good—and I caught hell for it from Mamaw, who was convinced that it was I who had led the innocent Queenie (and with a name like that!) astray. But love had sealed my lips, and I stood there with my head down, taking my scolding, while the hussy watched from a safe vantage, indifferently wagging her tail.

My gardening enthusiasm remained with me until it was pushed aside by more pressing interests when my voice went down an octave. It really wasn't until about twenty years ago that I rediscovered the garden's old seductiveness.

I realize in thinking it over that I'm an amateur gardener very much in the way I am an amateur cook. Both pastimes seem to be part of a larger piece—a kind of remembered secure and loving past. But gardening, for me, also has another dimension—it is good for the soul and puts things in perspective. There is something so right about what happens at each stage of an annual plant's life span that, when repeated over and over, it becomes almost impossible not to make the connection to oneself. It causes you to view the changes that come over you during your own span of years as part of a beautiful naturalness.

You won't find this to be a gardening book per se, but more a personal diary about a garden with some extra suggestions thrown in. I am not qualified to be a landscape gardener, nor do I hanker to be. The point here is really flowers—gorgeous and abundant flowers and how I like to use them, in and out of the garden. The photographs are meant to be enjoyed as they stand or as guides—and maybe inspiration for doing your own bouquets and gardening. I wouldn't suggest slavishly copying the photographs. Instead, express yourself, just as I express myself. My hope is that all this will be useful to you on two levels, then—a few gardening tips here, a few bouquet-making tips there. Result: lots of eye-filling pleasure.

One of the greatest things about summer country flowers is that they are so abundant, and the way you show them should take advantage of and reflect this. Even if you don't want to bother growing them yourself, they are in profusion everywhere. This lovely excess gives bouquets a certain look, a certain appropriate overstated quality. You'll find that even when vases are on three or four tables in the same room it's still not too much. What would look like a gangster's funeral during the winter looks just fine in the spring, summer, and fall.

Since this is a personal account, you will find omissions, in the gardening parts especially. And I have not grown all the kinds and varieties of flowers pictured on the ensuing pages. I did, however, attempt to make the flower selection as broad as time, space, and stamina would allow—and I had a field day doing that, literally and figuratively. I made some new friends and got some questioning looks while I was foraging for old blooming shrubs and certain kinds of flowers that I had seen here and there but didn't grow myself. I carried clippers and a bucket of water slopping around in the back of the car all season long, just in case I got lucky.

Because of the latitude in which I live (technically, Zone 7), and also because my house is so close to the ocean with its damaging salty winds, I cope with problems you might not have. Then, too, the time when various plants bloom for you may be different from mine. The best way to deal with this is to start when your daffodils bloom and follow the progression of flowers, ignoring the specific dates. The changes should follow pretty much as they do for me, once you are locked into your own "flower-time frame."

When I built my house in Bridgehampton, I really had had very little firsthand gardening experience (as an adult), and I made a decision then for which I am extremely grateful. It was one of those things, not quite whimsical, more dumb luck than anything else. At any rate, if you are just beginning you should think about it.

My property is only an acre and a half and had been a potato field for decades. What this meant was that I started with a blank and empty scrap of land—but a beautiful scrap, slanting gently down to the edge of a freshwater pond, affording a view out over the still water to the ocean. My decision to divide it into cultivated and uncultivated areas was good, if fortuitous.

The house proper I had built on a rectangular plot, which was planted in lawn grass, with a few flower beds cut into it. Railroad ties were buried in the earth around its perimeter to define it, and so a lawn mower could roll along them to keep the edges cut neatly. This set off the house and reduced the space that I had to keep up to something manageable. I bought forty black pine tree seedlings, each a foot tall, and planted them in a 2-foot grid just off the parking area. Several years later, I bought twenty-five more. This created a pleasing and strong visual impression, and also made it easy to water and fertilize them. After several years, I moved the small trees to their permanent places around the yard. In the process I lost only a few, and after five years they were as high as they would have been had I invested in much larger plants at the beginning (which I couldn't have afforded anyway).

The reason for this equaling out of height is the trauma a larger tree suffers when it is moved, which causes it to stay more or less the same size for the first couple of years. In the case of my own "field-grown" trees, this trauma was considerably reduced when I transplanted them because the move was quick and done under optimum conditions.

Meanwhile, the wild part became a meadow—a chaotic one perhaps, but it got right to work returning to what it had been before being put into potato bondage. Occasionally I would pull out something that I found particularly objectionable, but by and large I let it be, and took genuine delight in seeing nature reclaim it. Many varieties of goldenrod and wild aster appeared, along with black-eyed Susans and white daisies. *Rosa rugosa* took to growing along the water's edge and then leapfrogged into parts of the field. The usual cemetery cedars and chokecherries were brought in by birds—and finally an almost complete covering of bayberry. All of this was not only fun to watch and wonderful for birds, but provided excellent material for big bouquets.

After the first five years, I understood better what I was working with (including weather patterns) and felt ready to take a stab at the whole piece. Now, practically twenty years have passed, and the garden, though always in a state of change (which any worth its salt should be), is mostly under control. During this time I've had the joy of seeing it take shape, and have never regretted doing it as I did. Because I hadn't bitten off more than I could handle, I was free to enjoy it instead of viewing it with dread. Many projects founder before they have a fair chance to take hold because, in our enthusiasm (or anxiety), we misjudge the scope and difficulty of what we are embarking upon, and ultimately either give up or go humorlessly and doggedly on.

Of course, this sort of right-headed thinking has nothing to do with the seed catalogs that come in the dead of winter—making almost everyone order too many seeds. Here the pleasure of anticipation balances the waste of money. It's just a matter of learning when to zig and when to zag.

And to tell the truth, I did this book because I had to get it off my mind. For a long time, whenever I made a bouquet of flowers or weeds (you notice I didn't say "arrangement"—that's because I have never had any truck with "flower arranging," and probably no talent for it either) I would think what a beautiful photograph it would make. After working on my last two books, I also got to where I wanted to try my hand at taking the pictures myself because I had such a strong image in my head of how they should look. I finally decided to do a little book just for myself and guests to enjoy, but when I mentioned it to my editor, Carolyn Hart Gavin, she said, well, why don't we do it together. So here it is. It just grew.

One last thing: like most people, I wish I could more often be the person I sometimes am—and I am most often that person in the garden. So in many ways this book represents the best of me.

Bridgehampton, Long Island
Spring, Summer & Fall, 1984

LEE BAILEY'S
COUNTRY FLOWERS

APRIL

Overleaf: *April the first . . . the first daffodil of April*

APRIL

When the seed catalogs begin trickling in right after the first of the year, I start thinking of April. I take on that mind-set I remember having as a child when I was waiting for Christmas to come or for the start of summer vacation. To get me through this, I'll make several quick forays out to the house in the country—which is usually closed down for a few of the coldest months of the winter, looking dreary and forlorn. Most of my time there is spent scratching around in the mulch or leaves to see how things are surviving. As early as mid-January some daffodils have had the courage to poke the tips of their little green noses up to test the air. By April they mean business, sending fat dark green leaves up to receive the warming sun's rays. Rain starts to flood everything then, and you can almost feel plants growing. Montauk daisies have made tight little pea-sized buds all up and down their thin-barked, biscuit-colored stalks, and you can see the silvery clematis vine showing a touch of color, just waiting to leap out and commence climbing. Often, in a pile of tangled brown you can glimpse a regiment of small leaves thrown up by an annual that has reseeded itself. In protected areas, forsythia starts its spring explosion, to be followed shortly by those bushes in the more frosty exposed spots.

At some point each year I will say to anyone who will listen how amazed I am to feel the exact same thrill of expectation I have felt at this time year after year. Something about all this yearning to start, to grow, releases a sympathetic yearning in me. I inspect the garden every day, and when I have been away for a few days I'll usually take a little tour around it even before unlocking the house.

This is the month for getting ready. Days begin to warm quickly, even with the cold nights—so quickly, in fact, that I sometimes wish that what I have waited for impatiently would now slacken its pace. Suddenly there is so much to finish. I realize that with some things it is "do

it now or wait another year." If I don't move that privet to fill in a row before their leaves appear, I know I will stunt it, and it will just sit in the ground biding its time until next spring. I also realize that the ranunculus should have been planted last week, but with all the rain, it just couldn't be done. This is all familiar, all all right.

The most immediate reward is the appearance of daffodils and wood hyacinths, which start sparsely at first, then come in succeeding waves and drifts. I sit in the kitchen with a cup of coffee and just stare out the window at them standing stone-still in the first light of early morning. Sometimes I try to remember the name of a variety, and finally settle for taking a snapshot of it to paste in my garden diary a few weeks later.

As a matter of fact, April *is* daffodils. Their bulbs are a little bit of brown magic. (Any bulb is, for that matter.) By the time it is ready to be buried in the ground, a bulb contains everything it needs to produce a beautiful blossom. If you were to slice one lengthwise you would discover in the center of its creamy layers a tiny colorless flower ready to be painted by the sun, surrounded by all the nourishment it needs. A small miracle.

Although I like mixed bouquets, I prefer my daffodils straight. I'll mix colors and varieties, but seldom will I include other flowers (there aren't many at this time anyway) or greens. Generally, I pick a selection of the different varieties as they first start, and put each kind (or a small bunch of each) in a separate container—like a botanist doing research. Later, when they are nodding from every corner, I gather a basketful and enjoy the luxury of their numbers.

Then, miraculously, one week the rock cress is a mass of white, and the tulips are pushing up through the ground. I struggle to get the jump on wild sorrel, and start pulling out the long roots of wild carrot that have invaded a flower bed, doing it while the ground is wet. This is the month I have been waiting for. Here at last!

'February Gold' miniature daffodils blooming under a stand of pruned bayberry

'February Gold' miniature daffodils in an old brown glazed vase

The first viola of the season—its "baby picture"

The First Week of April

White Rock Cress

The First Week of April

One of the things I like best about keeping a weekly garden book is looking back over it to check on when particular plants bloomed and to recall the mood of the weather. This week I compared the same months for a number of years and was surprised how regular blooming times are and even how consistent weather patterns seem to be overall. (OK, maybe sometimes they are mostly consistently inconsistent.) But be it a dry year or wet one, a cool year or warm one, there is a reassuringly dependable basic rhythm at work. For instance, around the beginning of this month we always have a very hard storm filled with high winds and heavy rain—really damaging weather. This year, this week, we had an especially tough one, which didn't blow itself out until the next night. Winds were strong enough to give all the shrubs a good wrenching and to knock over large trees. In the wild, I suppose, this serves to rid forests of rotted and dead wood—Nature's way of pruning. But for the garden, it means repairing and extra cleanup. When a storm partially uproots a tree or shrub, I try not to despair. It's not necessarily the end. But I do get to work on it as soon as I can. The trick is to get it righted. I dig out from under the roots on the side that has been exposed, cut a few feeder roots if necessary to get the tree to stand straight, and then hold it in place with stakes so it looks the way a small tree does when it is professionally planted. After it is secure, I fill in the hole with soil and pour water around the tree's base until I am sure there are no air pockets, adding more dirt if needed. Then I mound dirt up over the side that was pulled out. Even if it has not been uprooted, only loosened by being whipped about, I still pack soil around the plant's base to give it stability and prevent further damage.

By now, daffodils are up, with buds showing on all but miniature varieties. Tulips are up too, but not as far advanced. The only thing that looks about to open is the bed of 'February Gold' daffodils, my earliest. I don't grow crocuses, but if I did they would have come in slightly earlier. Daylilies have about an inch of leaf, and there are a few heads of wild poppy unfolding. Perennial violas are in bud, too.

This is the week to start the cleanup. Taking first things first, I have the big limbs and brush from last year carted away, leaving smaller beds for another week or so, when it will be a bit warmer, and the perennials will begin to poke their heads out.

Plenty of other things could be done this week, but I think the best bet is to devote all the time to cleaning. I rake debris and dead leaves from around the daffodils so they will show off to their best advantage. Once the big stuff is out of the way, I can get after last year's dried stalks. Care should be taken here. If a dry stalk doesn't easily pull out, I use the clippers. You have to resist the temptation to yank or break these off by hand, because sometimes the plant can be partially uprooted in the process. I don't rush to pull back winter mulch from tender plants. This can wait until days, and especially nights, are warmer. And then I do it slowly—not all at once. A frost is still possible for the next few weeks.

If I have any spare time, I also try to take care of last year's pots and planters. With smaller containers, I remove old dirt and dead roots, starting all over. With larger pots, I take out dead roots and a good bit of soil on top and work in some new, with something like peat moss to lighten it. While I'm at it, I give them a shot of fertilizer so tubs will be ready to plant when I see something I like later on. Instant gratification. But if I get too busy, I skip it. This has a low priority.

It is amazing how much better even the brownest of landscapes will appear after being cleaned and raked. It inspires me to go on to the next step. But although things still can look pretty bleak outside, I can get some advance cheer by forcing spring-blooming shrubs. This doesn't take too much doing besides smashing ends of branches or slitting them so they can absorb water more easily. Since many shrubs you would want to force set their buds in the fall, you can give almost anything a try. Once the branches are prepared, put them in a warmish (not hot) spot in warm water. The buds will open and small leaves will appear in no time.

Here are some suggestions for things that force well. If you don't happen to have them in your garden, it might be worthwhile thinking of planting them with the early days of the season in mind:

WITCH HAZEL (*Hamamelis intermedia*). A particularly nice variety is 'Arnold Promise.' Order it from Wayside Gardens, Hodges, South Carolina 29695, or other sophisticated nurseries.

QUINCE (*Chaenomeles speciosa*). You will find the old-fashioned red ones in many places. Frankly, I'm not too keen on this color. There are better ones with more subtle colors to be had from Wayside. If you are going to plant one, go for a white or light pink.

FORSYTHIA *(Forsythia intermedia).* Even people who don't know anything about plants know forsythia. I really like the paler varieties, which make an "open" shape. A particularly nice variety is 'Spring Glory.' If you like the kind with spikier upright growth and really bright yellow flowers, buy 'Lynwood Gold.'

LENTEN ROSE *(Helleborus orientalis).* This is a popular and rather odd shrub. Take a look at it sometime if you don't know it.

This list is just a sampling, of course—more later.

I mentioned my 'February Gold' daffodils earlier; they have a lighter-colored relative, 'February Silver,' which is also very pretty. Also, aside from crocuses, don't overlook snowdrops. I'm particularly fond of them because they have such a strong childhood connection for me. (Even though we seldom saw snow where I grew up, I liked the idea.) Incidentally, always plant these little (or any small) bulbs in groups of least fifty. A hundred is even better. And don't mix the colors—they are too small to compete with one another. You want a drift of flowers.

Reminders

☐ Cut off old rose hips from last year and any obviously dead stems from roses, but leave them mulched a while longer. Always make your cut just above a bud.

☐ It's not too soon to plant sweet peas—and since you should never miss a chance to pull out weeds, you can do it when you are planting.

☐ Visit garden centers and nurseries regularly—to buy supplies and also to be inspired. When you go, buy rose systemics, fertilizers, twistems, labels, and waterproof pens. I also buy annual seeds as I see them, before all the best varieties are sold out. This is especially important if I plan to broadcast them for fall naturalizing. Some you might want a store of for that purpose are larkspur, cleome, and poppy.

☐ Start buying lilies now if you are going to grow them (all except daylilies). When selecting, buy ones that bloom at different times. Many packages will give you the approximate blooming dates as well as their height— which can be important too. Look lilies up in a catalog so you will have an idea of their range. Here are a few: 'Connecticut King' (clear yellow, 3 feet, blooms June and July), *Lilium auratum* (white with gold band, 3 to 4 feet, blooms July and August), and the tall August ones, 'Jamboree' and 'Imperial Silver' (5 to 6 feet). All of these are fragrant and easy to grow. Just make sure the soil is well drained.

'February Gold' miniature daffodils (Narcissus cyclamineus) are the first of my collection to bloom, usually starting around the end of March and continuing until almost the end of April. This long blooming period is probably due to the cool weather at that time of the year, which keeps the tender flowers from deteriorating.

The plant is small in scale, averaging 10 inches in height and is a good choice in a location where it can be seen up close—beside a doorstep or under a stand of small trees, as you see here, where it is blooming under my pruned bayberries. Because it is not very tall, care should be taken to plant them where they won't get lost in the tall grass. Incidentally, it has a charming twin called 'February Silver,' which has a yellow trumpet and white petals. They are equally hardy and can stand up to late-winter snowstorms. Zones 4–8.

When arranging daffodils, I cut the stems all to the same length. Here I have placed 'February Gold' miniature daffodils in an old brown glazed vase because I like the two colors together. The slightly bulbous shape of the vase allows the flowers to spread out nicely and naturally. After putting them in the container, I will sometimes (as here) cut the ones around the outer edge shorter so that these flower heads mask the stems of those behind them. But this is not necessary—I also like the look of stems. You can have it either way. Zones 4–8.

Viola plants are a wonderful investment because they self-seed or spread easily around the garden. They come in three basic colors (blue, white, and yellow), but there are now shades of apricot and maroon available. Buy them early from your garden center and keep them watered and fertilized in dry spells, and they'll keep going until very hot weather. They rest then and stay green, and return to bloom in early September. It's important to cut off the dead flowers so that the plant's energy goes to making new flowers and not new plants. Zones 4–9.

White Rock Cress (Arabis) is always the first mass of bloom in my perennial bed—a welcome harbinger. It is a choice plant for the front edge of a flower border, because it isn't rampant. But it does take on a pleasing free-form shape as it gets more established. After it finishes blooming (cut off the dead flower heads), it leaves a mat of low, silvery green leaves underneath, which makes a very nice ground cover. Plants are bought from garden catalogs or at garden centers, which, incidentally, often put plants on sale after they have bloomed. Zones 3–8.

Trout lily, or dogtooth violet, and glory-of-the-snow

'Hoop Petticoat' daffodils and 'Baby Moon' narcissus; blue grape hyacinth; two colors of 'Angel's Tears' daffodils—yellow and cream

Early tulip

The Second Week of April

Rainstorm coming

Celandine poppy

The Second Week of April

Since I still have Louisiana blood in these veins, and since the skies are apt to be alternately bright and cloudy for the next few weeks, I try to make the most of my time outside while it is warm. The temperature mostly stays in the chilly forties and low fifties. When I suddenly become aware of the sound of the ocean outside, I know the wind has switched directions and I switch sides of the house so I can work shielded from the wind. I hate to be cold. This is when I usually get to cleaning my small protected kitchen garden. Although this is where I primarily grow herbs, a few flowers are there—daffodils and irises, and later snapdragons. Several years ago I planted lily-of-the-valley in with the iris, and they seem to be comfortable together. Both are rapid multipliers and hardy. We'll see who wins; for the time being, it is a very pretty standoff. After edging the bed, I take a peek under the mulch and find a big mound of thyme and sprouts of tarragon. The sage is not out yet, but needs last year's dead wood cut. The first few shoots of lovage have made their appearance, as has lots of parsley. The curly type of parsley always makes it, but the tenderer flat-leaved Italian kind never does. There are also many clumps of sturdy chives. Makes me think how good a fluffy chive and cheese omelet will be for lunch.

'February Gold' daffodils have opened, and when I go back for a closer look, I discover wild geraniums beginning to come up under the bayberry and the first dark leaves on the tree peonies. And a sea of wood hyacinth leaves are pushing up through the needles under the pines.

Out along the drive, I can see tips of Japanese irises under last year's dried foliage, which I never cut off. And the first big shoots of wild orange tiger lilies. *Viburnum carlesii,* which will be filling the air with its marvelous scent next month, has put out small round flower heads and pointed leaves that are silvery gray—looking as if the whole plant, stems and all, has been spray painted the same color.

Weeds have begun to show themselves in the beds and are quite easy to root out—ground is soft from the rains. I get at this every chance I can. When I decide to go at them in earnest, I try to make myself as comfortable as possible. That way, I'll stick to it longer. I put on a couple of layers of clothes, which I can shed if the sun warms me and the wind stops. I also have an old pair of wool gloves with holes in the fingers, which are perfect for weeding. And, since my nose always seems to be running when I am out of doors this time of year, a good pocketful of tissues. I paint a lovely picture, don't I? You wouldn't know it to look at me, but I am as happy as a clam.

By the entrance to the house, there is a large wooden tub full of Johnny-jump-ups, all in bud. This reminds me that it is time to buy pansies and their cousins, violas. I always get a few flats from the nursery about now to spot around in the garden for a jump on the season. Those grown in flats are a few weeks ahead of the ones that have wintered over and so are in full glory when I buy them. Gives me a lift.

I have Montauk daisies, which grow well by the water—also large areas of *Rosa rugosa*. These all need to be cut down practically to the ground. If this is not done they tend to get out of hand, and become harder to manage each year. I'm ruthless with them, and they seem to thrive on the treatment. To add insult to injury, I never even fertilize them. They grow wild in these parts (and these growing conditions), so aside from cutting them back, I figure Nature will take care of them. Probably this is a good rule to follow with any indigenous wild plant that you might incorporate into your garden. I've certainly never pampered the bayberry, which I always seem to be pruning. I do everything the easy way if I can figure out how.

I noticed this week that the first small crested irises are putting up their narrow little leaves in the "wild" garden, and that the wild golden poppies are open. We are right on schedule.

I have several volunteer, or choke, cherry trees growing out toward the back of my property, and a single shadblow *(Amelanchier canadensis),* which got there somehow. The shadblow, which grows wild, has beautiful light gray bark in winter. The branches of both of these are good for forcing in the house. Another tree that grows in the wild and in gardens is, of course, dogwood. Forced, the flowers are a beautiful shade of green at the beginning. If you know anyone who grows azaleas, see if you can get them to give you a few branches. They make lovely pink flowers when forced, somewhat more delicate in color than when they open in the garden. I actually like them better this way.

The daffodils are really opening this week. Among the ones I recognize are 'Peeping Tom,' 'Tête à Tête,' *Narcissus tazetta,* 'Counselor,' 'Mt. Hood,' and 'Ice Follies.' I also saw, but don't grow, glory-of-the-snow *(Chionodoxa).* One good thing about doing this book is that I am forced to try to remember the names of the various varieties.

Reminders

☐ If you haven't pruned your roses back, do it *now*. The temperature will start changing rapidly now—although that is hard to believe sometimes, the plants know—and the roses will be leafing out anytime. Also check to see if any need replacing. Do this early enough so your nursery can get the varieties you want. You can also have pretty good luck with ordering if you do it right away—although this is better done in the fall. I especially like the "antique" strains from Roses of Yesterday and Today. Many of the rarer ones from this company almost have to be ordered in the fall, as they are usually sold out by spring.

☐ Inspect bearded irises for borers, which cause the fat rhizomes to rot in spots. If you find any damage, cut out the infected parts and burn them (never put them on the compost pile). Expose rhizomes to the sun. Only the bottom half need be in the ground. When feeding bearded irises, avoid manure (or rich soil), as well as excess moisture. And they don't want to be mulched. On the other hand, Siberian irises love all of the above.

☐ Remember that it isn't too early to be on the lookout for shrubs you want to buy at the nursery, especially an unusual or very popular variety that could sell out quickly. This happened to me for several years when I decided I had to have a pair of *Viburnum carlesii* plants. Every time I remembered it, it would be too late—all the best plants were gone. If you are not sure where you want to plant a shrub you buy, it can be stashed with its ball of soil covered with mulch until you make up your mind. But the sooner you get it in the ground, the sooner it will make itself at home.

The yellow flower of the trout lily (Erythronium) looks delicate but is actually very hardy, and blooms for a long time (about a month). When the flowers are gone, handsome foliage striped and mottled with brown remains for another month or so. The flowers are about 6 to 8 inches tall. Dappled shade and some moisture during dry spells are ideal. A mulch of pine needles enhances their beauty and helps keep their feet cool in summer. Zones 3–9.

The lavender blue flower of glory-of-the-snow (Chionodoxa luciliae) is especially eye-catching because the flower has a white center that makes it stand out. The painter Monet, who was a passionate gardener, planted masses of blue flowers in the shade of his trees and shrubs; he said they enhance the shadows. A nice idea. These are a good choice for this purpose. Plant as many as you can afford—a hundred or two at a time, all in one patch. Fertilize before and after blooming. Zones 4–7.

A collection of my first miniature bulbs, which I like arranged in individual vials and grouped together. 'Hoop Petticoat' (Narcissus bulbocodium 'conspicuus') is a tough little bulb with a long blooming period; it prefers a slightly damp growing spot and should be planted in groups of at least twenty-five to a clump, so they won't disappear when they bloom (it is only 6 inches tall). The narcissus 'Baby Moon' (Narcissus jonquilla 'Baby Moon').

Blue grape hyacinths are also tough and have a long blooming period. The small flowers that make up the head continue until all have opened, from bottom to top. They also spread rapidly.

Both colors of 'Angel's Tears' daffodils (N. triandrus albus) are about an inch in diameter, with two or three flowers on a stem. They multiply into large clumps very quickly and make fine cut flowers for small bouquets. All these bloom from mid-April on. Zones 4–8.

This was the first early small tulip to bloom. I couldn't resist cutting it so I could have a preview of spring in the house. Greigii tulips (hybrids and varieties of Tulipa greigii) stay in the ground for years, throwing out new flowers as they spread. These slightly smaller flowers have their own delicate beauty. Botanical tulips are a good investment for beginning-of-the-season cheer, especially in tubs on the terrace. Many can be forced to bloom even earlier in pots and then planted out in the garden to bloom the following year. Zones 4–8.

These hardy little poppies (Stylophorum diphyllum) grow out under my bayberry bushes, where they are partially shaded until after they bloom. Their foliage is pretty and remains after flowers have gone to seed—until about mid-July, when it begins to die back. Zones 4–7.

Midseason daffodils

The Third Week of April

'Robert E. Lee' daffodils

April winds kicking up the sand

My entire daffodil collection

The Third Week of April

I think that of all the weeks in the garden, this must be the toughest. Or so it seems this year, mainly because it is just more of the same—and not the kind of "same" that I am wanting. Weather remains changeable; I think I can sense a "right" change, but I'm not sure if this is only wishful thinking. Temperatures are still not warm enough to lift the spirits, but seeing the great mound of white rock cress suddenly covered with flowers helps. This is a very good plant to grow, because it gives you a splash of bloom when skies are still gray. And I console myself with daffodils.

The times when the pale sun has shone, I have worked on the clematis vines. Dead wood was clipped out. These are wiry vines, but care should always be taken with new shoots. And you must know your variety. Some want to be pruned because they bloom on new wood, and others would rather be left alone. Look them up in a garden reference book before you take to them with your clippers.

Toward the end of the week there was a single bunch of perennial violas (the pansy look-alike) that had budded out and the first dark purple flower opened—so dark it was almost black. On impulse I ran the trowel under it and took it into the studio to take its "baby picture"—trowel and all. After the picture was done, I stuck it back in its hole, and the rain began again. The little viola never even knew it had been immortalized. Before the rain started, I got some weeding done, and found many volunteers (violas) around older plants. This is their typical growing pattern.

I have been watching a long swath of hay-covered bed for signs of the first ferns, and finally saw several poking through—barely. I cleared around the ones I could find. But not too much. I like the way the fronds look against the mulch, so long as it is not all scattered about.

When the rains finally sent me indoors for good, I looked out the window and noticed that the trilliums have popped up around an old birch tree.

If it's blustery and conditions are too unpleasant to work outside, I use some of the time to check the houseplants and get them ready for the new season. During winter months, ferns tend to make rather halfhearted long growth, which I cut out so that they have a fresh start. They also go through a slight dormant period about now, which makes pruning appropriate.

A *Cattleya* orchid is in bloom on the windowsill of the bathroom. This plant, which was given to me years ago as a birthday present, blooms religiously every six months. I recall that some time ago I had the impulse to try orchids, but then I read about the special circumstances under which they must be kept. This so discouraged me that I didn't go on with it. Now I have discovered—as many of my friends have—that if cattleyas are allowed to sit undisturbed in a sunny east window where they get a bit of humidity from the shower or steam in the kitchen, they require nothing more than a little pruning now and again and plant food. I've never had such luck with the other varieties of orchids, however.

If you still are in the mood to force a few branches for the house this week, don't overlook the possibilities of tree flowers, especially maples, which have an odd and complicated bloom. And then there are the flowering cherry trees. When forced, these often reward you with a pretty good facsimile of their later spectacular blossoms. Prunus is a very large genus, with more than four hundred species, many of them cherries. A few you might want to be aware of are 'Kwanzan,' with double pink flowers, and 'Mt. Fuji,' with double flowers too, but in purest white. This particular tree is low-growing, about 15 feet. There are autumn-flowering cherries as well, which sometimes bloom twice.

And last, don't forget magnolias. This is probably the final week before they open naturally. They are unlike other blossoms for forcing, in that you should wait until a sliver of color shows before cutting them. Some varieties are tougher than others, but none is tough enough to grow in my location. There are two kinds that I see around: star magnolia is the first to bloom, and has loose, relaxed flowers of white, which are slightly fragrant; saucer magnolia, or tulip tree, which we call purple magnolia in Louisiana, comes about a week later, with tulip-shaped flowers that start as dark pinkish purple and get whiter as they mature (don't we all). Both are extremely hardy and have the advantage of looking elegant in the winter, with graceful limbs and gray bark.

I planted trout lilies for the first time last year, and they are coming up. I don't know what took me so long to get around to them, because they are beautiful flowers and despite their delicate appearance are very hardy. You may know them as fawn lily or dogtooth violet. They grow to about 8 to 10 inches and produce a bright yellow flower with turned-back petals. If you have enough, they make nice small bouquets. Like all small flowers, they should be planted in groups for best effect. Mine seem to be about a week behind those I have seen in more protected areas.

A little farther away a patch of miniature daffodils has started to open. They are called 'Baby Moon' and are particular favorites. I also have a daffodil called 'Kissproof' blooming. I've never understood how they came up with that name.

Also blooming are some of the daffodils with pink trumpets. One of the oldest varieties is 'Mrs. R. O. Backhouse.' Since she came on the scene in the thirties the hybridizers have been working overtime. Try some of these; they are beautiful.

Reminders

☐ The next time you take a swing around the garden, check vines that are tied to supports to make sure they are secure—this goes for the supports as well as the vines. If a trellis is wobbly, make an effort to get it stabilized before the vines put out their growth. If you must repair a trellis that holds clematis, it is a good idea to put a brick at the point where stems come out of the ground so you won't damage them. This is where clematis is most vulnerable.

☐ If the weather cooperates, most garden seeds can now be planted. While the seeds are germinating, keep them damp. Even with all the spring rains, wind dries out soil quickly.

☐ I like Mexican tuberoses in pots and in the cutting garden for late summer bouquets. They are such slow starters, I try to get them going in pots on a warm windowsill about now. Give a few a try. They don't make a very elegant shape, but one stalk will perfume a whole room.

☐ Nurseries are getting in their roses now. When buying them, look for well-shaped plants to start you off on the right foot. Buy several 'Iceberg' plants. They are one of the strongest whites and bloom freely all summer. I was also reminded of another beautiful rose when I saw the plant there: 'Queen Elizabeth.' This is a tall one, about 4 feet, and a generous bloomer. Lovely clear pink flowers.

Pictured here are 'Mrs. R. O. Backhouse,' 'Pink Glory,' 'Louise de Coligny,' Scheeper's 'Pink Beauty,' and Bourgondien's 'Satin Pink.' I started planting these daffodils with pink trumpets seven or eight years ago and add a few each season. They are a breed apart, and mine all seem to bloom about a week later than their more conventional relatives. The mother of them all seems to be Narcissus *'Mrs. R. O. Backhouse,' which a friend told me was listed in a Scheeper's catalog in the thirties for over thirty dollars a bulb—during the height of the Depression! It is a good idea to buy ones that appeal to you (as many as you can afford) when*

you see them, because they seem to come and go rapidly. For example, in 1980 Wayside Gardens offered a page of five pinks, but by 1983 they were down to two, with one new entry. Gone were 'Mabel Taylor' and 'Pink Supreme'—and, worst of all, 'Mrs. R. O. Backhouse' herself (although the latter continued to be available in the Van Bourgondien catalog). Zones 4–8.

Narcissus 'Golden Ducat' is a sport of the old favorite, 'King Alfred' (of which I'm not too fond). 'Erlicheer' and 'White Lion' are both very fragrant. The truth is, you are either a doubles person or not. These three are among the aristocrats of their class. The only problem is that their heads can be so heavy that they are more susceptible than single varieties to breaking under their own weight during a hard spring rain. But worth a try.

The simple single narcissus is 'Orange Wonder.' Its orange eye makes it distinctive from a distance in a mix of blooms. It also puts out three or four blossoms at a time, which adds a bit of looseness to a bouquet of doubles. Zones 4–8.

Once a season when all (or almost all) the daffodils are in bloom, I pick a few of each variety to put in one big bouquet— kind of like a class picture. To make such a bouquet in a container that doesn't hold water (like this basket), first line it with heavy foil and then fill it with soaked bricks of oasis. Essentially, oasis is a very lightweight, extremely absorbent plastic that is sold in pieces about the size of a brick. After soaking it in water, stick the flowers into it— where they will stay. The brick gives them water; your container won't require any more. Most florists will sell oasis to you. Among the flowers here are Narcissus *'Kissproof,' 'Roulette,' 'Mt. Hood,' 'Binkie,' 'Duke of Windsor,' 'General Lee,' 'Ice Follies,' 'White Lion,' 'Golden Ducat,' 'Pink Beauty,' and 'Silver Chimes.' Zones 4–8.*

This is the first daffodil that I bought from a catalog and planted at my house. From that small purchase, probably no more than twenty-five bulbs, I now have hundreds, which I have separated and moved several times. It naturally is one of my special, sentimental favorites. I usually pick the first few to bring inside to enjoy. Van Bourgondien refers to it as being most likely the 'World's Favorite.' It is called 'Sweet Harmony' by Wayside, and 'Oklahoma' by Scheeper's, which no longer carries old 'Robert E. Lee.' The point is that there is great similarity among them all, even if they are not exactly the same, so you shouldn't worry too much about the name. Buy the ones that catch your eye at the garden center, or order by catalog. A very early version of this bicolor, which was mentioned previously, is 'February Silver,' a fine strong bloomer—although not as large. Zones 4–8.

The Last Week of April

'Spring Glory' forsythia and box elder

Purple magnolia, as it is called in the South, or saucer magnolia

'White Czar,' a bicolored violet

Flowering dogwood

The Last Week of April

This is the week when it happens. There is finally no place left for the water to run off into. The ground is as full of it as a watermelon—and then it is finished. The rain stops. Sunshine takes its place, drawing living things, plant and animal alike, from the earth like a magnet. Winter gray has yielded to pale green. Daffodils, except for the very late varieties, have all opened, sending forth a subtle sweet breath and wave upon wave of yellow, jumbled with shades of pink and orange. The family of cardinals has reappeared, as they have done for the last decade. I catch a streak of red in the still bare bayberry.

In this short seven days the clematis has leaped forward a good foot, it seems. And the bleeding hearts have done the same. Even the most cautious plants find the renewal irresistible and start to drop their winter protection. Suddenly there are buds on all the tulips, where there were practically none the last time I looked. And from nowhere the first cream-colored one has opened.

It was time to plant sweet peas several weeks ago, "on St. Pat's Day," they say around here. I never got around to it, but it's not too late. I ordered an assortment of seeds for cream and white ones, which I'll accent with a couple of mahoganies and shell-pink colors. To plant sweet peas, dig a trench about spade deep and fill it with compost (or fertilizer) and loose rich soil to a couple of inches from the top. Place seeds in a row an inch apart and cover with two inches of soil. Press down. Leave the top of the trench recessed so that when you water in hot weather (it's coming) it will accumulate where it is needed. Now is when you should have your trellis and netting in place for the peas to twine on. The tall ones smell sweeter than the knee-highs.

At about this time I begin to notice small seedlings that have volunteered where annuals grew the year before. Lots of dark violas and Johnny-jump-ups are scattered around, as always. But sometimes I will find only one or two of less hardy varieties. These determined little fellows are always special favorites of mine, because I fantasize that they have chosen to grow (for me). So I treat them with care. It is easy to learn to recognize shapes of leaves of various seedlings, and a pleasure to find them. Some of these transplant well, such as calendulas, which will be coming on later, and the violas, which are very sturdy. Others, such as larkspur, California poppy, and mallow, are difficult to move, so are best left where you spot them.

Dead wood had better be cut out of hydrangeas now, before buds start popping. I have a number of old blue ones that started out white; the minerals in the soil decided on blue instead. My grandmother used to put nails in the soil around hers to intensify the color. She swore it worked. I'm not sure.

I pull all the mulch from the roses, work fertilizer and rose systemic into the soil, and water them. It is only about two more weeks until the first aphids, and you want to be ready for them. Follow the directions on the box when using systemics. Incidentally, take a look at the pruning job you have done on the roses. Remember that the center of the plant should remain somewhat open. If the air can circulate freely around branches, they are less likely to develop mildew. And it will keep molds from getting a head start.

'February Gold' daffodils have about had it. However, they remained in bloom for almost a month. It is so cool when they start that they last longer than any of my others except for the miniature variety 'Peeping Tom,' which will go on for another few weeks. And do they multiply!

No buds on the bearded irises yet, but they must be about to form. Lily-of-the-valley is sending up slender stems with tiny buds, and many of the other very early daffodils are finished. The old large trumpet varieties seem to be the first to bloom and the first to finish.

The garden is so filled with flowering shrubs in bud, which are only a few days away from blooming, that there is really no need to try to find things to force. Just bring in a few ladened branches and they will open naturally inside along with those outside. Or maybe a day or so quicker.

This week will likely just about mark the end of the daffodil season—with just a few stragglers left over for the beginning of May. My white 'Thalias' are still going, along with 'Amor.'

I have several primulas in a soggy spot in the garden out by the pump house. They need to be kept watered, and this is about the only place that stays damp naturally. If you have such a spot yourself, try them. Their flat little clusters of bright flowers are very appealing, and they come in a number of colors. Another flower in bloom now is candytuft. This is especially satisfying for a perennial border, and it lasts for several weeks.

Tulips are just now beginning, with one or two of the very early varieties open. There are even earlier ones, which I don't grow. I've seen the short Greigii hybrids in bloom in some gardens, as well as 'Plaisir,' which is red and white striped, and 'Cape Cod,' which is apricot with a lemon yellow edge. These are all very nice with daffodils out in the open, if you are not cursed with the rabbit problem.

Reminders

☐ Be on the lookout for interesting geraniums as they come into the nurseries and garden centers. Even if you are not quite ready for them, you had better pick them up when you see them. They tend to go fast, and later on you are likely to be stuck with only the most ordinary varieties to choose from. If they have not been hardened yet, keep them in a sunny room until you can be sure the weather is not going to do them in. If they are on display outside in the slat houses of the nursery, it is likely to be OK to leave them out in your garden.

☐ Flats of alyssum and some of the tougher annuals are also arriving. It is really a bit too early, and planting them in bloom can give the garden an artificial look. However, if you see something rare that you want, by all means buy it. Set it in the mulch, in a spot that is easy to water, until you can get around to planting.

☐ It should be safe to plant in the garden primulas and hyacinths that were bought as houseplants. As a matter of fact, this is how I came by the few primulas that I have. Fertilize and water them and they will bloom again next year. There is no use trying this with paper-white narcissus, however. They don't make it. But you can put potted lilies out later on, if you have any of these. They do very well. (That is how I came by the Easter lilies I've got growing.)

Johnny-jump-ups (Viola tricolor)—*a form of pansy that almost always has a bit of yellow mixed with the blue in its flower—have been stuck into oasis in a foil-lined basket. This would be a dull task if you were making a larger bouquet, but so early in the season, when flowers outside are still scarce, it doesn't seem like too much trouble. These flowers self-seed at such a rapid rate that they are considered almost weeds by some gardeners. Obviously, though tiny, they are tough.* Zones 4–8.

The flowers of the lovely Forsythia 'Spring Glory' *are not as overpowering as 'Beatrix Farrand,' which is sturdy and stiff in shape. The best way to buy these common shrubs is to pick them out at the garden center when they are in bloom. Watch for a graceful shape. Although some problems can be overcome with pruning, it is best to get off to a good start.* Zones 5–9.

The box elder (Acer negundo), *according to gardening expert Donald Wyman, should be considered a weed tree, seeding everywhere, broken easily in storms, and it has no autumn color. But it certainly has interesting flowers, so pick it at the roadside but don't buy it for your yard.* Zones 3–8.

The flowers on the pale gray branches of this tree (Magnolia soulangiana) *open before the leaves appear. A small tree (approximately 15 feet), it was supposedly created by one of Napoleon's retired generals around 1820 by crossing a* Magnolia denudata *and an* M. liliiflora. *It has a mild fragrance and keeps well in warm water if the branches are deeply slashed. Incidentally, these trees do well in the city.* Zones 5–9.

Viola odorata *'White Czar' is a descendant of the common sweet white violet. In flower lore, the violet symbolizes modesty. When making a little bouquet of fine-stemmed flowers, always cut them to the same length, and then place them in the container all at once so they will support one another. Violets grow best in leafmold or rich organic matter, and benefit from extra watering in summer. They spread with abandon and should be planted only after careful consideration. Cutting them back in July when their leaves begin to yellow and look tired causes them to send up fresh leaves. They can then also use a bit of fertilizer to help them along (soak first, then add fertilizer, to avoid burning).* Zones 4–8.

These cuts of dogwood (Cornus florida) *were forced. I especially like the flowers' greenish cast when they first open. As happens out-of-doors, these get whiter as they mature. I placed them in a tall glass cylinder because I like to be able to see the whole branch. This is one of spring's finest small trees—or was until a few years ago, when it was acknowledged that they are subject to borers and a condition called "dieback." Where they are really healthy and happiest is in dappled light provided by taller trees, such as oaks, or on the edges of woods, where they are protected from the hottest summer sun. When homeowners plant them in hot, dry, and airless places, they die. They also don't much like strong winds or salt air—which is why I have none. Japanese dogwood* (Cornus kousa) *is replacing the American dogwood because it is hardier and resistant to problems.* Zones 5–9.

Salvia

Snapdragon

Zinnia, one of my favorite flowers

Eustoma

How to Use a Coldframe

Scabiosa

Verbena

Cosmos

How to Use a Coldframe

To tell the truth, I have never used a coldframe, but so many of my friends who are avid gardeners have recommended them to me that I'm going to give one a try next year.

Although they can be used to grow lettuce and other quick-crop leaf vegetables, and to store plants, I am primarily interested in one for starting seeds. As is the case with most things in gardening, you learn best by doing. So my advice to you (and myself) is to just plunge ahead.

By planting seeds early you have seedlings in their second leaf almost ready to set out in the garden about the time you would just be planting seeds outside. This means you have gotten almost a six-week start on the season. I know there are so many garden centers and nurseries around that sell prestarted seedlings that you might wonder why you should bother, especially if getting larger plants in early is not too important to you. For me the reason is simply that although many plants are available, they tend to be of rather unimaginative varieties and of limited color selection. For instance, I am very partial to big ivory-colored zinnias, because they are marvelous in bouquets. Of course, they are impossible to find prestarted. On the preceding page are some flowers I think would be excellent for a coldframe.

In essence, a coldframe is an enclosed patch of earth with something over the top that will let the light in and concentrate heat that passes through it—creating conditions like those outside in the spring. From what I have read, these devices have a long and interesting history. The Romans brought the idea to Britain when they set up business there. For people used to the climate of Italy, the chilly winds of England must have been hard to take—especially because the fresh fruits and vegetables that were part of their natural diet were not available. To remedy this, the Romans set about digging pits that faced south (this southerly orientation is important when selecting a site; east is second best), to catch as much of the sun's light as possible, and then covered them with sheets of mica or talc. Although the light that managed to filter through must have been meager, it was still possible to produce an out-of-season crop this way. They also discovered that it was possible to raise the temperature by incorporating fresh manure underneath the plants in the frames and then raising and closing the lids to regulate the heat buildup.

Coldframes were refined over the years and became a basic part of all English gardens, large and small. They remained in general use up until the First World War, when most of the great estates lost their crews of men and such luxuries went by the boards—being replaced by systems that were easier to manage. Today on old estates you can often spot rows of these frames, which were customarily built of blocks sunk 2 to 3 feet into the ground, filled with weeds and looking neglected. The average frame was about 3 feet wide and 6 feet long, and the glass sashes (sometimes old window frames) were very heavy. Each morning the gardener would have to remove huge and cumbersome mats and then crack the sash for a bit of air circulation in the frames. At night the process would be reversed. Of course, in cold weather nothing was opened. Sounds tedious, doesn't it? Probably it was. And probably it woud have been enough to discourage me. But it's not for nothing that we are now living in the Age of Aquarius (whatever that is), in which all things are rendered simple. Such simplicity in this case is due to a mechanism, not requiring any electric current, that automatically opens and closes the coldframe top when the inside temperature reaches a certain level.

While it is comparatively easy to make a coldframe from scratch if you are even moderately handy, they can now be bought in kit form from companies like Burpee and Parks for about forty dollars, or delivered ready to go for approximately twice that. They are usually 3 by 4 feet and made of redwood so they won't rot, with a plastic top, which won't break and isn't too heavy. You will need a cheap thermometer to measure the temperature inside the frame, and about ten bricks to hold the whole thing down. If you don't want to look at it when summer comes, it can easily be stored, being light.

Once you have decided on the kind of frame you are going to use and have selected a sunny site facing south, prepare the soil by digging it deeply and lightening it with peat moss and a little sand. Work in some fertilizer and you are ready.

The next step is learning by doing. Just as when sowing seeds outside, different varieties have slightly different requirements, which you discover as you try them. Even if the conditions are not perfect the first time, you are likely to get usable results anyway. Just don't plant seeds too thickly (this will make them leggy), and don't let them dry out if the weather gets hot and the top opens a great deal. As a rule of thumb, you can plant most seeds about six weeks before you would normally do so in the open.

When seedlings have formed their second set of leaves, they must be put either into larger flats or into peat pots. Or they can be reset in the coldframe if there is room. Some plants will do better if they are pinched back to make them branch out. This must be done after they have become established. The next step is to harden them to outside temperatures by leaving the frame open for longer periods of time during the warm daylight hours. This is done the final week or ten days before they are moved out into the garden.

I think you could learn how to manage one of these frames in a single season. I intend to. And while learning, don't invest in anything too expensive. Get to know the ropes first.

MAY

Overleaf: *Tulips opening in my cutting garden: 'Golden Artist,'*
'Zwanenburg,' 'Ace of Spades,' and 'Court Lady'

MAY

May is the month my sanity returns. It's then that I shift gears and come to terms with the possible. All during April an intoxicating state of ebullient planning has me. But with the first string of really warm days, which bring out the great rolling wash of bright green, I suddenly realize we are *in* the season. This realization sets me straight and settles me down. Enough impossible schemes and fretting about being behind on my work plan. I make the schedule, so I'm on schedule. With so much to engage the senses, it would be foolish, if not downright ungrateful, to waste time thinking about what won't get done this year.

If I had to choose a single flower that symbolizes this month for me, it would be the tulip. The climate where I spent my childhood was too warm for them to grow naturally—bulbs had to be refrigerated and pampered for months before they could even be planted—and so I never saw them in the profusion I have become accustomed to here.

I suppose everyone has heard something about the lunatic period in Europe in the seventeenth century when single bulbs sold for as much as three thousand dollars. This must certainly be the height (or depth) of horticultural foolishness. The mad trading went on for a time, and then all came tumbling down, causing the Dutch government to step in and take control of the whole shebang. Interestingly, the bulb business (and it is *big* business) is still controlled by the government, much as the French control wine and De Beers does diamonds.

Cultivated tulip bulbs have about five centuries of recorded history behind them. The first Lily-flowered ones are said to have been taken back to Vienna from Constantinople in the middle of the sixteenth century by Holy Roman Emperor Ferdinand I's ambassador. From there they got to the Netherlands, where Dutch growers fiddled with them, coming up with doubles and rounded petal varieties as well as ones with twisted shapes, now called Parrots.

Tulip bulbs are unusual because they generate new varieties constantly in a process called "breaking." A bed of ordinary cultivated tulips will suddenly throw out a completely new variation, and even new colors, seemingly just for the hell of it. We now know that breaking is caused by a virus. The odd fellows it causes are called "sports."

Funnily enough, as fond as I am of tulips, I don't much like them in a border or formal bed. They look a bit too rigid and architectural to suit me. I want plants to meander around and take a more irregular form in such settings. My tulips go in the cutting garden for bouquets rather than in the yard to be looked at.

By the time the brief foggy period comes at the end of the month, when air and ocean are trying to agree on a temperature that suits them both, the tulips in my garden will be finished. Unfortunately, their bulbs have to be lifted out of the ground and stored if they are not to "run out" and become smaller as they begin to multiply. I'm too lazy for this and just let them go. Since they are cut flowers to me, I find the smaller and odder flowers they begin to produce past the second year quite appealing. After four years or so, I just turn the bed over and fertilize it. Without even bothering to remove the old bulbs that are exposed in the process, I start with new ones.

There is always an exception. A friend sent me a bunch of bulbs from Holland over ten years ago, which I planted around a birch tree that sits next to the entrance to the house. All, except one, disappeared years ago. The holdout is clear yellow and puts up only one flower each year. It grows in a protected spot and is always the last tulip to fade. I don't particularly like it where it is, but I'm reluctant to disturb it. Such determination has to be respected.

The First Week of May

The last daffodils of the season to bloom

Blue skies, the first day of May

The First Week of May

This is the week for serious weeding and edging the beds. By now all perennials are showing themselves, and the weather is more stable.

I have found that thoroughness at this point really pays off later. Often shoots on weeds belie the root system underneath, especially if it is one like wild sorrel or wild carrot, which winters over. I never just pull off the top leaves, but try to get the roots out. In the case of something like sorrel, this can be done with fingers and a claw, but with the ones that make a long root, such as wild carrot, a trowel is necessary to dig the roots out. If you fail to do this, the plant will only come back stronger than before. Fortunately, after all the rain the ground is easier to work in.

When I have finished the bed, I give it a good covering of mulch, using pine needles, because I have lots of pine trees. Large nuggets of pine bark apparently are very popular these days, but I think they look awful; they make the ground look as if it is covered with prunes. On top of that, this mulch can't be worked into the soil successfully later. If you like pine bark, use it finely shredded. Also successful as mulch is straw. Make sure it is clean—no weeds. In case you don't know, the purpose of mulch is to keep weeds down—the ones that get through are dispatched with ease—and to retard drying, from which exposed soil suffers very quickly. The first year of weeding a new bed is the toughest. After that you get the upper hand, so keep plugging.

The first daffodils are beginning to fade, so I cut the heads off and give them a reward of bone meal. I sprinkle it around their base and do a bit of scratching with the rake. I don't make a big thing of this. Daffodil and narcissus beds are shifting from yellows to creams and whites, spotted with dots of bright orange and the palest yellow. My whites and creams are the last to bloom.

Tulips are all showing color, except the very latest blooming varieties. They will come into bloom very quickly now. When they start, I like to go out early in the morning to have a look at them as the sun slants through their wonderfully colored petals.

There are lots of buds on the wood hyacinths, but no real color yet. The first flowers have opened on a beautiful patch of wild geranium out under the bayberry, and the last of the miniature daffodils have made a pool of light yellow alongside them. These small varieties are very sturdy, lasting longer than some of the bigger and showier ones.

Vibernum carlesii is almost open. A few of the small individual flowers already have started opening in several of the heads, sending out a wonderful sweet-spicy fragrance. Sadly, this lovely plant is subject to graft blight disease as it ages. Newer and more dependable hybrids are beginning to replace it, such as *V. burkwoodii, V. carlcephalum,* and *V. juddii.* They are all fragrant, but none lives up to this old-timer. Plant one close to a bedroom window on the south side of the house and be rewarded.

Wild chokecherry blossoms are just about ready. This is the perfect time to cut them and bring them into the house. They are a particularly nice pink color when they first open, which fades as they get on. Also, they can be messy to clean up after, if you let them stay too long. Three days is about enough—but worth it.

Another group of plants that is showing color is *Dicentras,* known as bleeding hearts. I think I like the traditional ones best of all. They make such graceful curving stems of flowers, which last for weeks. There is another common variety with beautiful silvery gray foliage, which makes a perfect foil for other plants, blooms all summer long, and will thrive in sun or shade. I also have a few whites, which complement the others.

I've noticed lots of quince coming into flower in the yards. It is a plant I've never had, because I don't much care for the shade of the flowers (in the common variety) or the shape of the plant itself. I think if I had one, I would give it a good pruning in the center to make it into an interesting form.

I took a walk in the woods this week and found many things about to open. Too early for dogwood, but the ferns are beginning to unfurl. Wild geranium is also just beginning, whereas mine is already in bloom. I saw wood violets and lady-slippers around the tree stump, and wild lupine just putting out its spires of buds. There are a couple of weeks yet to go.

Reminders

☐ When forsythia finishes blooming, it is time to tend to the lawn. Apply preemergent crabgrass killer. Discuss this with the owner of your garden center or nursery, and be sure to follow the directions on the label. A really healthy lawn has good resistance to weeds, and you might want to skip this if you are organically minded. I'm personally a little bit in the middle of this whole thing. Organic gardening is like natural childbirth to me. It sounds right, but if I were the mother I would probably be doubtful about depending on it entirely. Anyway, remember that this is also the time to seed bare spots. When doing this, spread seeds beyond the spot so it will all blend together nicely.

☐ Label your bulb locations. This way, you will not have any confusion later on when you want to plant after foliage has died off and you have cut it back. Also, this is helpful if you should want to move anything or to fill in any places that look somewhat sparse. It is amazing how easy it is to forget where things are.

☐ If you like fruit blossoms, but don't want to damage the crop of a young fruit tree in bloom, look for an old apple tree. They are by far the nicest of all, in both color and fragrance. They can be found growing along the road (more often than other fruit trees) or on a piece of land that was once occupied by a house. Their old bark is beautiful in color and often has a pleasantly rough surface. When you bring the branches inside, don't forget to pound the stems so they can get plenty of water. Cut them before they open fully or just when they start. The foliage of these trees is a very nice powdery green, and is also lovely to look at.

☐ Continue to keep an eye out for bedding plants. I do this every week until I have what I want. I also find things from time to time that I hadn't expected to see. Many nurseries and garden centers get their new stock on Thursdays and Fridays, so get there early if you can swing it.

☐ If you find that there is a type or color of bulb plant in your garden where it shouldn't be, act now. Dig it up, with a big clump of dirt, and transfer the whole thing. Water it, and let it die back naturally. It will survive and be fine next year.

Several years ago I planted about twenty-five bulbs of these miniature daffodils, called Narcissus 'Trevithian,' under the bayberries. You can see how well they have spread and naturalized. This may be due to the fact that their foliage has been allowed to fully ripen each year, which is probably the most important step in daffodil culture. Remove the untidy foliage too soon and the bulb has no way of receiving nourishment. Zones 4–8.

I don't really know what any of these daffodils are called. They were all dug up from an old garden in back of a tumbled-down barn when I first built the house. The bulbs had been there so long that they were almost a foot deep. Whatever they are, they are always the last to bloom every year. Zones 4–8.

My favorites, the "black" tulips

The spectacular 'Ivory Floradale' tulips

Cream-colored and green-striped tulips

A basket of my brightest tulips

The Second
Week of May

The Second Week of May

Something spectacular happened this week. I went back to the cutting garden on Monday morning to have a look at the tulips there, which I knew were very close to blooming. It was time to make plans to photograph them. They were all standing unmoved by wind, with swollen buds, but none had opened except the early cream ones, which always are first. I made a mental note after inspecting them that I would start the pictures next weekend. The following morning, as I was driving out past the garden, I caught a flash of color from the corner of my eye and backed the car up to check what it might be. I was startled to find that the tulips had all opened during the night, except for a few Parrots and Rembrandts. What a glorious sight—and what a lot of work in store for me! As it turned out, I didn't get a chance to use all the colors I had planted, because there were just too many. Tulips picked in the morning, directly after they have opened, will last in the house for almost ten days—as compared with three or four days for the ones bought at a florist.

The lilacs are all in bud now, with just a few individual flowerets opening in the heads. I am especially fond of them at this stage. The colors are so rich, and of course, if you cut them at this point they will last much longer. When you grow lilacs, particularly the common "lilac-colored" one—which incidentally is lovely—keep the area surrounding the plant cleared of the suckers that come up around it. These shoots will finally obscure the mother plant, creating what is to me an unattractive and lumpy mass in the garden. The hybrid varieties are not quite so bad on this score.

As the daffodils are finishing, leaving only a few of the white ones spotted around and a patch of the miniature 'Baby Moon' under the bayberry, lots of other things are about to begin. I noticed first buds on the roses in a protected area of the deck. Unfortunately, the first aphids had noticed them too. But just a few, so the systemic is working to some degree. I need to give them a shot of rose dust. Buds are appearing on the irises, and I see that slugs are at work on them in a few spots. This is especially true where debris has collected, which gives them a damp spot to hide and live in. These slugs can be extremely destructive, cutting down newly planted seedlings completely in several days. In the case of the irises, I merely clean the area carefully so that air and sunlight can get in. For seedlings I sprinkle a bit of "slug bait" around them when they are planted. But it is a continuing problem.

White rock cress in the beds has now been replaced by a beautiful display of perennial candytuft. The daylilies' foliage is growing very lush, so when I am out feeding the narcissuses and daffodils with bone meal I give them a generous feeding as well.

While driving around, I see many flowering trees, the most spectacular of which are the showy 'Kwanzan' flowering cherries. These are extremely popular, but I must confess I find them too excessive, almost vulgar. (I suspect you are beginning to get on to me and my partiality toward the less hybridized flowers and plants.) It seems to me that so many of the hybrids, which over the years have been manipulated by the breeders and growers—who seem to be obsessed by size and brightness of color—have mostly succeeded in creating specimens that don't really look at home in the landscape. They are like a glamorous movie star, larger than life in a modest little play, that seem to unbalance everything by their presence. The best thing about cherry trees (if not movie stars), however, is that they get to be quite large very quickly. But you should at least check out the options available to you before committing yourself. The best way to go about this is to visit the nursery *after* reading your reference books and your garden catalogs. Cherries are referred to as *Prunus* in these books.

The smaller crab apple trees are more to my liking. These reach a height of 20 to 30 feet under good conditions, and their branches are beautiful in arrangements as well as in the garden. Of course, some strains are better than others, but over the years a few have developed susceptibility to fire blight, which requires destruction of the tree, and a disfiguring scab that requires spraying by a tree man. This is just a caution. The good ones are wonderful. Among them are Sargent's crab, with pink, almost white, flowers. It is a wide-headed kind that seems more horizontal than vertical and is lovely to look at even in winter. 'Katherine,' a deep pink, double-flowered one, opens almost white and reaches a height of about 20 feet. There is a weeping variety (a form I'm not crazy about—except in willows—again, too much tinkering) called 'Red Jade,' which was developed by the Brooklyn Botanic Garden. I mention it because it makes dazzling red berries after its white blossoms fade and is really tough.

I bought and planted white snapdragons and dark purple salvia plants (the purple is an interesting color in the salvia, although I don't particularly care for it otherwise) and some *Eustoma,* which carries the common name of prairie gentian. You could grow snapdragons and salvias from seeds, but in my climate you almost have to buy prairie gentian plants, because they require so much time to germinate and grow before they bloom. They are annuals, but are native to warm areas, where they reseed themselves. The ones I put in will be for August flowering.

Reminders

☐ If your clematis is not out by now, you had better start thinking of replacing it. This should be done while there are still good selections around and so that the new plant will have plenty of growing time. I have a number of the old reliable ones called *Clematis henryi,* which are quite hardy and produce big white flowers in June. There is a fragrant white fall-blooming one that is also hardy and will grow about 30 feet in one season. It's called 'Sweet Autumn.'

☐ Plant the annual seeds you sent away for. Each year I put in snow-on-the-mountain, which is very pretty in bouquets, and 'Everett Dirksen' and white marigolds. I have a friend growing white Italian sunflowers for me. I've also gotten seeds for green zinnias and large light pink ones, as well as ivory and white. The other colors I'll find around. I'm also partial to the little 'Persian Carpet' zinnias. These are similar to ones called 'Old Mexico,' but I like 'Persians' better. I stick seeds for the common single nasturtiums around in all the beds. I'm one of those people who even like their odor, although I never cook with them. When planting annuals, be sure your beds are properly cultivated and fertilized and then follow the instructions on the packets. Keep soil damp if possible, and look out for slugs and other pests when seedlings start coming up.

The so-called blacks of the tulip world are actually dark purple. For this bouquet, they were all left the length they were when they came from the garden, with leaves attached for bulk. First I laid the flowers in a pile; then I put them in the large-mouthed crock all at once and moved them around. I especially like the way the Lily-flowered ones with the pointed petals, called Tulipa 'Burgundy,' flop around. The ones with ragged petals are 'Queen of the Night,' and the other is 'Ace of Spades.' I love them all. Zones 4–8.

I used the tulip leaves to make this bouquet. The stems were all cut the same length, with the leaves attached. Then, all together, they were put into the mouth of the vase. The leaves hold them in place and make an interesting design. This particular Darwin hybrid, Tulipa 'Ivory Floradale,' doesn't hold up but a year or so in the garden—becoming smaller each season. The new Darwin hybrids don't run out as quickly, but unfortunately their colors are not nearly so subtle. Zones 4–8.

Sturdy-stemmed, creamy white 'Zwanenburg' tulips are mixed with 'Court Lady,' which carries a green stripe on the petals. All are stuck into oasis in a white glazed oval container. Zones 4–8.

The handcrafted basket was lined with heavy foil before being filled with bricks of soaked oasis to hold the flowers in place. The reddest ones are Lily-flowered. This particular one is named 'Marigot,' the bright pink and green is 'Greenland,' and the salmon pink is 'Pride of Zwanenburg.' Zones 4–8.

Wood hyacinths blooming under my pines

Volunteer chokecherry

Money plant blossoms

The Third Week of May

Sweet-smelling lily-of-the-valley

Sweet-smelling viburnum

Lilacs and bleeding hearts

The Third Week of May

With tulips at their height, there isn't much room for anything else in the house, but I came across a luxurious bank of lily-of-the-valley, and couldn't resist picking a handful. They are such beautiful and fragrant little flowers, and in a big patch, doubly so. The ones I found had originally been planted in one of the old cemeteries that dot our landscape here on eastern Long Island. Judging from the headstones, no one had been put to rest there in many years, so this patch might be a half century old. Although they had obviously been planted around a marker, they had long since migrated out beyond the surrounding fence and all up and down the banks of a drainage ditch. I wondered how many people ever notice them. The flowers are so small that they aren't very visible from the road, and the cemetery itself is so old that it isn't visited often, except by caretakers and an occasional tourist. It is always a joy to come upon naturalized plants. And you never know where this will be.

Azaleas and rhododendrons are now beginning to show color—a good time to buy them at your garden center. Azaleas are very popular in the South, and I remember seeing some in a garden once, that had been beautifully pruned—giving them a marvelously interesting shape. The variety was the common old magenta one, which makes quite a large mound if left uncared for. But these particular ones had been clipped to reveal their basic structure, very much the way apple trees are. The result was that blossoms were carried in large tufts out at the ends of long graceful branches. Azaleas are not too successful in my location, near the water, so I have never tried this, but it is something that I would recommend doing. I think it would work with rhododendrons as well—another plant that can use a little help with its shape.

When choosing azaleas, you should be careful about selecting colors. They can so easily clash with one another and other plants in the garden if your scheme is not planned properly. For balance there is a fine white, lower-growing one called 'Delaware White.'

Incidentally, like many other villages in the Northeast, Bridgehampton had beautiful American elms planted along its broad streets. Sadly, these magnificent trees have mostly succumbed to Dutch elm disease, but a good substitute tree is *Zelkova*. It has small leaves (not much to rake in the fall) and is hardy with a good shape.

My *Viburnum plicatum* 'Mariesii' is in bud now, a beautiful variety. This genus of plants is quite extensive and one that you should investigate if you haven't done so already. They are mostly very hardy and give you great armloads of flowers. Some varieties worth looking into are: *V. dilatatum* 'Erie,' *V. sieboldii,* and the smaller *V. opulus* 'Compactum.' They also grow very quickly.

This is also the week of the dogwood. These delicately shaped trees can be seen in wooded areas in many states. They are as beautiful when they are first opening as when they have made that gorgeous display of white—occasionally punctuated with a shade of pink. It is worth a drive out to the woods just for a glimpse of them. When I went out for a walk this week, I saw that the wild geraniums had come into bloom since my last visit, sprinkling the ground under the dogwoods with bright pink.

Under my own pine trees, wood hyacinths have done the same, but with blue—a beautiful sight. These little bulb plants are perfect for under trees, because they love shade. For effect, you must plant a large quantity in an area.

All the clematis is now filled with buds. These vines grow furiously for a month or a little more, but once they start to make buds, all forward growth stops. That is why it is important not to break or damage these first shoots—they are all the real growth you will get for the whole year. Anything after the blooms fade is minimal.

Many buds on the bearded irises now, same with the Siberian, but nothing so far on the Japanese—which are the last to bloom. Japanese irises, unlike bearded ones, respond very well to bone meal applied early in the spring. It is also very important to keep them weed-free.

If you grow dahlias, tuberoses, and gladioluses, now is the time to plant them. Tuberoses and gladioluses will pretty much take care of themselves, but dahlias need a little more care. When you plant them, choose a very sunny spot that is well drained but close to a source of water, so they can be watered with ease. If you are going to grow the tall varieties, buy 7-foot stakes in advance. After cultivating and fertilizing the soil, dig holes about 2 feet apart and a foot deep. Drive stakes in *hard* with something hefty, like a sledgehammer. These will support the plants as they grow. It is important to do it now, before the tubers start growing. Obviously, if it is done later you run the risk of damaging them—because for the stakes to be effective they must be very close to the plants. These plants become quite heavy, which is why it is so necessary that stakes be well anchored. Now carefully inspect the tubers and find their tiny green shoots (maybe only half an inch in size) and place each in the hole, shoots toward the sky. Gently cover with about 2 inches of good soil. As stems grow toward the light, keep covering them with soil. Water at least once a week if the season is dry. Also fertilize with any good all-purpose fertilizer. They are greedy feeders.

Dahlias have been grown in Europe since 1789. Like the tulip, they have an exotic history. There was a great deal of secrecy about them when they were first discovered by Spanish explorers, who wanted to keep them away from the French and English. Finally, however, a Swedish botanist named Anders Dahl was able to get enough plants together to hybridize them, and the plant is consequently named in his honor. Eleanor Perenyi, in her wonderfully entertaining book *Green Thoughts: A Writer in the Garden,* tells the tale, along with many more, although this one might be apocryphal.

As your tubers grow it's important to tie them loosely to their stakes so that they don't collapse under their own weight. At the end of their growing season, let the tubers mature in the ground. They must be taken up in the fall and stored in a cool, dark, and dry spot for the winter if you live in a cold climate. If you do this, they will last for years.

Reminders

☐ Keep weeding and mulching. Also, now is the time to plant dahlias, tuberoses, and gladioluses.

☐ Try to get the last of your seeds in this week, if you can. We often have a bit of rain at the end of this month, and I like to have seeds planted so they will have the advantage of this good soaking.

These beautiful little flowers grow in the shade and multiply rapidly. Endymion hispanicus, *wood hyacinth, used to be called* Scilla hispanica *or* S. campanulata. *The flowers are approximately 10 inches tall but can get up to 15 inches. These are planted in an ideal place, because they can be left to run wild. They will grow almost anywhere and once they start are almost impossible to get rid of—so be sure you know where you want them. There are blue, pink, and white varieties. Zones 4–8.*

Just a few branches of this will be sufficient for a bouquet. Trim the lower part and pick them in bud when they are the pinkest. Choke *or* wild cherry (Prunus virginiana) *is widely distributed between Newfoundland and North Carolina, mostly brought in by birds. It is considered a weed tree, and it flowers briefly. Its fruit is not edible. Some came up close to my property line, and I left*

them there as a windbreak and pruned them. They look pretty good. Unfortunately, tent caterpillars like them a lot, so I have to be on the lookout for the first signs of these pests in the spring and give them a good spray of insect killer when they first appear. After a few years, the caterpillars will give up. Grows to a height of 30 feet.

*The money plant, or honesty (*Lunaria annua*), grows 3 feet high on sturdy stems. Its flowers can be lavender, purple, or white. Pick them before the sun comes up and let them stand in tepid water for a few hours before putting in a vase. If they are large, split the stems. This is one of the best plants for the casual gardener, because it's there for keeps and doesn't need much care. It prefers some shade and is slightly fragrant. The rounded, translucent seed pods are often used in dried flower arrangements. Zones 4–8.*

This is the wondrously fragrant Viburnum carlcephalum *('Fragrant Snowball'). To make this bouquet in a container with a wide mouth, I had to put a plug of oasis in the top to hold the flowers in place once I had them in. This hybrid is the winner of many awards from England's Royal Horticultural Society and reaches a height of 6 to 8 feet. Everybody should have one. Like all members of the family, it's extremely tough and, once established, will last a long time. Zones 5–9.*

I use a vase with a small mouth because the stems on these flowers are so slender. Hold them together and put into the vase all at once. I added the leaves as an afterthought. Lily-of-the-valley (Convallaria majalis) *is an excellent ground cover (but goes bald in winter, if you care). It even grows in partial shade. It can benefit from a heavy mulch of leaf mold in winter when the ground is frozen, but is hardy enough to make it on its own. In flower lore lily-of-the-valley signifies "return of happiness." Zones 3–9.*

These are the common kinds of lilac, Syringa vulgaris, *and bleeding heart,* Dicentra spectabilis. *Two old favorites. The lilac has been here since the seventeenth century, brought by early settlers as a souvenir from home. Today there are over five hundred varieties of the shrub. Both plants are lovely in the spring, but the bleeding heart dies back, and the lilac foliage is not the prettiest. Lilac, Zones 3–7. Bleeding heart, Zones 3–9.*

The Last Week of May

The Last Week of May

A few years ago I got the notion that I would like to try to naturalize cosmos and cleome in an area of my yard, as a friend had done. After turning the soil over and raking out the roots (quite a job) I generously sprinkled it with seeds. These came up and bloomed beautifully, so I thought I had it made. Unfortunately, the wild daisies also liked this newly liberated area and were much tougher, being native to this locale. The second year they took over, and I finally had to give up the fight and let the daisies have it. I did add foxglove seeds, which came up with no trouble and were able to hold their own. I have also put in a collection of lilies from White Flower Farm that they say will naturalize—if the rabbits don't get them all first. I had to face the fact that cosmos, as lovely as they were, would have been too hard to maintain. In gardening you must admit when you have been beaten—you retire gracefully. Actually, the bed as it is now looks just as pretty as the other did, and so the "compromise" was painless.

In another week or so, I'll have to start cutting the ripe foliage off the narcissus and daffodils in the beds. (I don't bother too much with this out in the meadow.) This can become a bit tedious. I discovered, by planting daffodils in with daylilies out along the driveway, that the luxuriant growth of the lilies comes up and obscures most of the daffodil foliage about the time it is ripening. A good solution. In back of the bed of daylilies I have planted a row of bearded irises, and in back of this a row of Japanese irises, so I have a continual unfolding of flowers up until the middle of July—and beyond (sporadically) from the daylilies. Speaking of daffodils, the last two white ones of the season have just faded, as have my

tulips, although there are later-blooming tulips that I don't grow, such as 'Blushing Bride' and 'Tender Bride,' both of which are white with pink edges. Chokecherries and all the other fruit trees have also shed their petals. If they don't get washed away by the rains, these fallen petals are very pretty on the ground for a day or two.

I mentioned foxgloves earlier. It is interesting that the ones in the wild bed are all practically in bloom, but the ones in the cultivated beds, which are much larger, are only now putting up buds. When using foxgloves in cultivated beds, it is important to understand their growing pattern. They will remain in the same place for only a few years. Older plants will ultimately die out, but in the meantime a few younger ones will come up in the vicinity of the mother plant. These should be left as they are, so you can transplant them when you remove the original ones—or, better still, left in their new location. This moving and spreading is one of the most appealing things about these perennial beds to me. It keeps their form from becoming static. You must always be prepared to accept the changes and encourage plants, which tell you by their growth pattern where conditions suit them the best. Fill in any holes with annuals, many of which, like calendulas, will reseed themselves for years.

The dogwood continues this week in all its glory, as do the wood hyacinths. An old reliable dark purple iris looks as though it will be the first of its species to open. There are buds on all the irises now, so we should have quite a display in the next few weeks. The foliage on these plants is nice even after the flowers have faded. It lasts up until August.

Almost all the plants in the perennial beds are showing color. Among my favorites are coralbells, which are delicate and best used in front of a border and in masses because otherwise they don't have much impact. We will get into the making of a perennial bed or border in more detail a little later on. The bleeding hearts are also continuing, beautiful and hardy—and, surprisingly, because they look so fragile, they can take a lot of wind and knocking around. The more familiar of the old kinds, *Dicentra spectabilis,* is the largest but dies down during the summer. When this happens it is important to mark it with a small stake so you won't mistakenly plant over it. I find it helpful to keep snapshots of the beds to remind me what I have growing in various places.

If I have any seeds left that I bought in my first flush of enthusiasm in the spring and didn't plant and don't know where to use, I broadcast them in the bed with the daisies and foxgloves. Sometimes a few will come up and bloom—never quite as they would be if they had been cultivated, but a nice addition to a mixed bouquet during the height of summer.

Reminders

☐ Buy your annuals before they get too big in their little planting cartons. Ideally they should be about 2 inches high, not blooming dwarfs, which they become if left unplanted for too long. Before planting them, check to see if they have become too root-bound by taking them out of their cartons. If this has happened, cut off the bottom quarter inch of roots and snip off their tops (about half an inch) and get them in the ground fast. Give them a generous amount of water. This brutal treatment will encourage new bushy growth, which will start to come in very quickly.

☐ Thin and transplant some of the seeds you planted earlier if they are in their second set of leaves and about 2 inches high. When handling them, don't pick them up by their stems. Instead, pick them up by their leaves, between thumb and forefinger. Keep seedlings damp but not soaked. Water gently with a spray, not a blast of water. Finally, don't let a hard crust form on the beds where they grow. Cultivate them gently. Remember, they are still tender.

☐ Discard any tulips or daffodils (on a compost heap if you have one—I don't) that don't please you. Gardening is a ruthless game. Get rid of colors or plants that you don't want as soon as you get a look at them. I planted some double tulips that turned out to have awfully heavy heads (overhybridized). All broke in the wind and rain that are a part of the weather pattern here each year, so out they went.

☐ If you grow chrysanthemums, and are a traditionalist, pinch them back. I grow only two plants (of the same color and variety) and prune them the way a nurseryman told me to do years ago—by whacking off the whole plant to about 6 inches from the ground with the shears. This must be done before buds start to set. This "technique" works fine for me, but I must admit that my lone variety of chrysanthemum is an ordinary and therefore tough soul.

☐ Now that you've had a chance to see all your tulips in bloom, be sure to make careful notes of which you prefer and, if you have time, of when each blooms and its approximate height. Amazingly enough, it is quite easy to forget this simple information after a few months. And it is the sort of thing you will want to know when you are making your selection for the coming year. Since these are cut flowers, you don't want them to be in bloom all at once if they can possibly be staggered a bit.

☐ While you are making notes, you might record a few observations about your daffodils while they are on your mind. Although unlike tulips these are planted for a lifetime, it is also helpful to know when favorite varieties bloom and also when the ones that have finished their cycle have matured enough to have their foliage cut back. These notes will also point out to you which beds might need an infusion of new bulbs to balance their blooming period.

I am not really too certain what any of these tulips are. The tall ones are Rembrandts, but they are from bulbs that have been in the ground for several years and have started "breaking"— which makes them attractive to me. The smaller ones in the little pitcher are really a mystery, because they are the kind of flower you get after about the third season and don't bear much resemblance to the originals. Zones 4–8.

At the left are Cottage tulips (Tulipa viridiflora 'Golden Artist'), about 11 inches high, which last quite well. They were all cut to the same length before being put into a narrow-mouthed pot with a bulbous lower half, which allows them to spread out. Beside these is a lone sport, which is interesting to see close up. There are always one or two of these in every batch. Since this breaking is caused by a virus, it's best to keep them segregated in the cutting garden. The pink Parrot tulips on the right are called 'Fantasy.' I left the stems of these longer and of varying lengths. When tulips are not closely packed in a bouquet, they will move around, responding to the light—which can be very attractive. The taller pink and white tulips in the back of the picture are a variety called 'Blushing Bride.' If you like tulips in mixed perennial beds, these are easily assimilated, because they are less "exotic" than the others in the picture. Zones 4–8.

A perennial border in lush bloom at the end of June

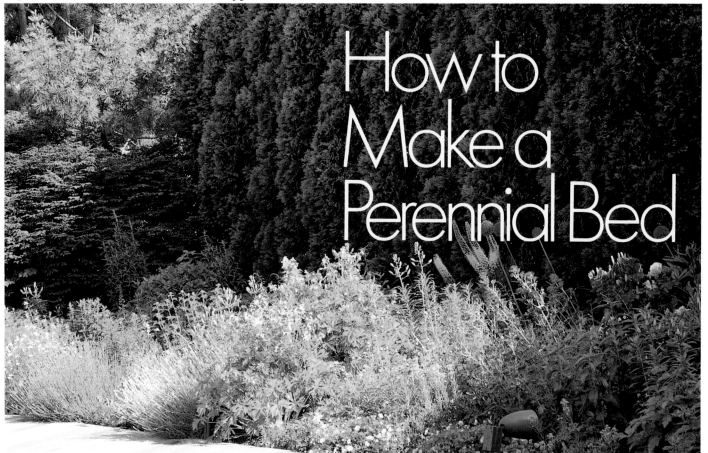

How to Make a Perennial Bed

A closer look at the perennial border

How to Make a Perennial Bed

Maybe this section should really be called "How to *Start* a Perennial Bed," because it is a process that is most successful if stretched out over several years. Although you will have, of course, situated the bed where it can be looked at and enjoyed with ease, this method does not mean you will have to look at a sparse and underdeveloped flower patch during the time it is filling in. More on that later, but first:

Plan to prepare the soil in the fall when you want to plant the following spring. It should be deeply cultivated. There is something called "double-digging," which you have probably heard mentioned. To double-dig a bed you must simply spade down about 18 inches (in trenches) and reverse the soil, putting the top half in the bottom of the trench. If the bottom half is poor soil, it is discarded and replaced by a rich composted mixture. Maybe this is more than you can handle; if so, you can still get good results if you dig down about a foot and improve the soil with peat and compost or fertilizer (manure). It is best to do this in the fall so that it will have the winter to settle back down. Cover it with a good layer of salt hay and start doing your research.

It is a good idea to make a rough plan on paper of what you want. This will help you to visualize it and will be a handy reference. And be cautious—plant sparingly the first year. Give yourself time to get the feel of what you are doing. Check out a good basic book or two from your library, such as *Low Maintenance Perennials* by Robert S. Hebb or the one on perennials in the Time-Life series. You are going to learn as you go along, so expect to have a few things not work as you envision them. This is just part of the game (and the fun). To remedy the problem of the bed's looking too sparse for the first couple of years as it takes shape, you merely fill in with annuals, which are available all spring at your nursery or garden center. You will have less and less need for them as you go along.

Using a good catalog, such as the one from Wayside Gardens, take a look at the following, which I call major perennials (that is, they stay put once they are planted and shouldn't be moved): peony, gas plant, daylily, balloonflower, old-fashioned bleeding heart, and Siberian iris (which does need dividing every five years or so—so should be placed where you can easily get at it). The equally beautiful, but less permanent, perennials are: columbine, flax, baby's breath, lupine, delphinium, pinks, coreopsis, Shasta daisy, phlox, foxglove, hollyhock, false dragonhead, Oriental poppy, bearded iris, Japanese iris, campanula, and yarrow. There are many others, but this is enough to get you started. Because you cannot learn about all the flowers in one season, this is another good reason for going slowly. Incidentally, by saying that this group is less permanent I mean that they require more work, either dividing, pampering through the winter, or just because they plain give out after a couple of years.

Next, to quantities. Suppose you want a bed roughly 10 by 4 feet, and you are in residence all the time, except maybe for a few weeks in summer. You will want something in flower the whole season, and attractive foliage in between. A basic bed this size, which must be situated where it will have three or four hours of good sun each day at least and where it will enhance the view, can manage: one peony (June, 3 by 3 feet when grown), two white *Dictamus* (June, 2 by 2), two daylilies (July–August, 2 by 2), three clumps of balloonflowers (July, 8 inches square), two bleeding hearts (May, about 10 inches square each), one clump of Siberian iris (May, 2 by 2), and one clump of monkshood (August–September, 2 by 2). This bed would run itself for years, but would look pretty spare and dull for the first few seasons. This is where the minor perennials, which generally grow faster, come in, along with the annuals. So add these to your basic structure.

Once you have made a rough plan and prepared the bed, order or shop early in the season, when plants are freshest and you have a selection. Your bed will need turning over with a pitchfork and will benefit from another shot of manure or compost then. Try not to walk on it any more than necessary, because this packs it down. Next, set out your plants on the ground where you want them to go, placing them according to how much space they will ultimately require. If you can visualize what they will look like full grown and in full bloom, so much the better. For an "island" or freestanding bed, walk around it

and get a view from all sides. Be aware of the height of the plants and place taller ones in the back, if the bed is against a fence or hedge. For island beds, tall plants go in the middle and graduate out to the front edges according to height. Set each plant in a good-sized hole and firm the earth around it so that there aren't any air spaces. Do this all in one day and then give it a good, deep watering. Finally, mulch it with a thin layer of salt hay or pine needles.

The next step is to fill in. Visit your garden center or nursery regularly and buy plants as you see them coming into bloom. You can move things around if they get a bit overgrown.

Now this is all I am going to tell you because I don't want to scare you off with too much information. There are many, many more perennials than the ones I have mentioned. There are also tips about pests and insects and fertilizing and watering and weeding and on and on. But these are not really specific to a perennial bed. Just use what you have learned about the rest of your garden and your common sense and plunge ahead, as I suggested you do with the coldframe in the last chapter. You can't go too far wrong in any event. At worst you will have to move or replace some plants. You will probably overplant in spite of what I may say, and then it will be a process of eliminating. Don't be afraid to dig up and discard a plant you don't like or a flower that is the wrong color at the wrong time. There are lots of other possibilities.

Remember to ask questions! At the nursery, at the garden center, of fellow gardeners who have had the experience. By next year you will be able to answer others' questions.

 *A selection of flowers picked from a perennial bed at the end of June.* Left to right: *spires of blue salvia; white astilbe; yellow lily* (Lilium); *red Jupiter's beard* (Centranthus); *yellow daisy* (Anthemis); *Japanese iris* (I. kaempferi), *in two shades of blue; yellow spire of the foxtail lily* (Eremus); *tall pale blue agapanthus; red feathery astilbe; low blue scabiosa; white peony, with a pink one in the back* (Paeonia).

A blanket of ferns

The lady-slipper orchid

Wild sarsaparilla

Wood anemone

Wild columbine

A Walk in the Woods

Joshua Green

Wood betony

Wild blue lupine

Pink campion

Bird's foot violet

A Walk in the Woods

I have friends who go for regular weekly tramps through the woods. However, I have to confess that, as much as I like the out-of-doors and nature in its natural state, I seldom join them. But at either end of the summer season, the thought of such excursions is magnetic to me. It is then that I find the woods the most beautiful and mysterious.

Often I will take a little solitary hike at the beginning of May after the weather has brightened and while plants and wildflowers are just beginning to show themselves. This is slightly early, but I usually can't wait. At least I know where to look when I go again toward the end of the month. By that time, lots of things are up.

One of my breathtaking discoveries was the great blanket of ferns you see on the previous page. What a splendid sight they are in all of their uniformity and quantity, stirring ever so lightly in the breeze.

Many wildflowers are easy to miss because, unless they have naturalized into a large patch, their simple flowers don't call attention to themselves. And many of the very earliest ones are of such modest colors that they almost blend in with the dried leaves and twigs surrounding them—particularly the flowers growing in the richer loam and rotted leaves. Maybe they are so contented with the richness of their surroundings that they don't need attention. In poorer soil and under what would seem to be awfully unwelcoming conditions I many times find plants like phlox, lupine, and bird's-foot violets making large splashes of color—where the earth is almost too mean to support a good crop of weeds. This year in such a circumstance, I came across something I had never seen before and took a picture of it. I couldn't recognize it in any of my reference books, but our local wildflower expert told me it was indeed rare—at least in these parts. It turned out to be a variety of wood betony.

I always enjoy trying to spot lady-slippers. These seem to grow equally well in both rich and poor areas. They were unfolding around a partly rotted tree stump early in the season, and later I saw a great quantity of them mixed with lupines on the gentle roll of a bank leading down to a dried-up stream bed.

To me, the woods are always at their best in the very

early morning, with the sun slanting through the overhead branches and dispersing the mists. Of course, this means things are pretty wet underfoot, so I wear tall boots and an extra sweat shirt.

These outings have the same effect on me as being on a small boat early in the morning. That is, as soon as we are under way, I am starving. I remember being on a little fishing tub out of Marigot, on the French side of St. Martin in the Caribbean. We left just at sunrise, and the captain's wife had made sandwiches of big chunks of cheese and hacked-off pieces of French bread. We finished off the whole batch of them—washed down with tepid beer—by 8:30 A.M., and were as happy as if we had good sense. Well, anyway, I always take along a sandwich or two (usually egg) and a little Thermos of hot coffee or tea.

In the fall, the wooded paths have a completely different magic. Although there are particular areas that are noted for their spectacular fall foliage, even places with a more modest showing can be lovely and worthwhile.

The lady-slipper orchid or moccasin flower (Cypripedium acaule) especially likes a woodland environment and can be bought commercially, but is very particular where it will grow. It is an endangered plant in the wild and should never be picked or dug up. Zones 3–8.

The wood anemone is easily cultivated in the wildflower garden. When established, it resembles the wild strawberry. Zones 5–8.

This wild member of the Aralia family has rhizomes (underground storage stems) that are usable as a substitute for sarsaparilla. It grows from British Columbia to Newfoundland, south to Georgia; west through Tennessee and Illinois to Missouri, Nebraska, and even farther westward, according to Audubon. In other words, everywhere.

The columbine (Aquilegia) is a member of the buttercup family. This one has an unusual combination of yellow sepals and red-orange spurs. There are many domesticated versions of this in a wide range of colors. They are interesting in all white, too. 'Silver Queen' is one such variety that is sturdy with a long blooming period. Zones 4–9.

The wood betony (Pedicularis) is a rare plant that grows from Manitoba to Quebec and south to Florida and west to Texas. It is a member of the snapdragon family. Lousewort is its common name, which comes from the Latin word for louse, and refers to the misconception once held by farmers that cattle and sheep would become infested by lice if they looked at it—an odd notion, considering the beauty of the plant.

Pink campion (Silene caroliniana) grows in open woods and is related to the garden pink. Zones 5–8.

Lupine grows by the roadside all over America. Texans call it bluebonnet, and it's their official state flower. Another form, which grows to 6 feet and has yellow flowers, is native to California. There are other smaller and colorful versions everywhere. It's a member of the pea family and flowers in open sunny places. Unlike peas, its seeds are poisonous if eaten.

Bird's foot violet (Viola pedata) gets its name from the shape of its leaf, which is distinctly and deeply lobed and looks like a bird's footprint. The flowers are a fine clear blue. A woodland aristocrat that's now being made commercially available by better nurseries, it does best in poor soil with dappled light. Zones 4–8.

Overleaf: *My favorite small rose, a hybrid Macrantha, Rosa 'Raubritter.' It has one long blooming period, and the beautifully shaped flowers, which open in clusters, never lose their shape. Hardy, it can grow to a height of 7 to 9 feet. Zones 4–9.*

JUNE

When I graduated from grammar school, our class sang a song that began something like "'Tis June, the month of roses . . ." I remembered that the other day, for some reason. That song must have been written by someone around here, because in Bridgehampton in June roses are everyplace you look—falling over fences, growing along the pond and the roadside, popping up in the meadows. And, of course, standing at pruned attention in neat yards.

But let me get back to that graduation for a minute. No one that day seemed to notice or care that roses actually bloom in April in Louisiana. Maybe our teacher thought it was somehow more civilized or tonier to live where roses bloomed in June. To add to the general nuttiness of the graduation festivities, our class did a little dance around a Maypole (in June, the month of roses). I recall my mother was thrilled that I got through it so well. I think my father was mostly puzzled.

Anyway, roses we got here—beginning with the wild rugosas down by the pond and then the old-fashioned 'Inspiration' climber in a protected area on an inner deck. A few days later all hell breaks loose in the rest of the garden. I like the older varieties, the ones with gentle colors, strong fragrance, and seemingly hundreds of petals. When they bloom the air is full of their perfume.

But before the roses, there are the bearded irises. The few white flags (which is what we called the common white bearded irises when I was growing up) are the first. Next are the big blackish purple ones. I got on to dark-colored flowers with a gift iris a few years ago. Before that I used to think such colors were merely tricks. Now I love them. Their magnificent tones are so spectacular in the bright sunlight—almost the only situation where you can really see and appreciate the subtlety and variety of their dark beauty. When these finish, we have the Japanese irises, and someplace in between are the Siberians.

I sometimes think this is the most satisfying month of the season. That is because the whole garden is at its freshest. The green is brighter and all the growth is so lush. And, of course, flowers start opening in waves as the month progresses—one kind after another. You also get the full impact of all your efforts, from both the end of last season and your work earlier in the spring. It is a time full of rewards for the senses, and the weather to enjoy it all with.

Speaking of weather, this is when we really seem to go in for extremes—chilly mornings for a few days when it is invigorating to work outside, then, just as suddenly, a week that seems more like August than June. These extremes require that you take a few precautions—but more on that later.

Toward the end of the month, daylilies have sent up their long slim stems and a few of the earlier ones have even begun to open for a preview of their July show. It is then too that wild daisies are at their best, covering meadows with great drifts of speckled white. And the foxgloves, which I have managed to naturalize in several wild areas of the garden, start popping. They, like wild daisies, are tough enough to hold their own with the weeds that consider these areas their own preserve. At one time I thought I might be able to get the same good results with cleome, because it seems to be such a tough plant. Unfortunately, success with naturalizing them has always eluded me. They germinate quite well, but by the time they are ready to go, they seem to be overwhelmed by the faster-growing plants, which deprive them of light and crowd them out. Too bad; their tall flower heads, which keep growing and getting longer, would have looked just right after the foxgloves and daisies. I suppose the lesson here is that in order for plants to compete, they must have a root system that will at least partially winter over, so that they can start growing earlier and keep their heads in the sun. Another plant that naturalizes quite well for me is the yellow tickseed, coreopsis. The rabbits love them, but coreopsises are tenacious and keep trying until they get ahead of the game.

'Love with Lace' iris

'Joyce Terry' and 'Dutch Chocolate' irises in the perennial bed

'Prince Indigo' iris

A mixed bouquet of bearded irises

The First Week of June

A bed of 'Pink Taffeta' iris

The last tulip of the season

Irises blooming by the dining deck

Bronze 'Spartan' iris and 'Cosmopolitan' iris

Early morning, early June

The First Week of June

When I first started planting bearded irises it took me several years before I accepted the conditions that nature lays down in my locale. Each season, just as they were coming into flower, we would have several days of heavy rain, which more often than not was accompanied by strong winds blowing off the water. The wind wasn't cold, but it had enough force to knock down a number of the longer stems of iris, and the heavy rain would invariably fill the flowers on these graceful stems, making them top-heavy and the wind damage worse. Shorter varieties didn't exactly thrive on such treatment, but managed to get through it all right and straighten themselves up after a day or two. During their first three years, my tall irises seemed to be growing perfectly, multiplying happily and sending up lush foliage and numerous buds each season. Maybe it was this that made it hard for me to see that no matter how they might pick themselves up, the long-stemmed varieties were doomed to be knocked down and broken each time just as they were starting to open. And I would always be disappointed. Finally I caught on and moved all the long ones to the protected areas, leaving their shorter brothers to weather the winds. It makes me think of the many times I have tried to ignore or fight nature's cycles instead of working around them. A good lesson to learn.

Obviously, that came to mind this week when we had our usual windy rainstorm. As you can see from the pictures, we are now in harmony. One piece of advice about this is to cut off the water-laden and damaged heads as soon as the rain quits, so that the stems can be righted and remaining buds can open properly.

All these bearded irises are once more just about to open, and I'm sure I'll wake up to a beautiful display of them one morning next week. Although the dark purples come first in my garden, it is only a matter of days before they have been joined by the others. Purple Siberians are also just about to bloom now, and will be followed in a couple of weeks by the whites.

I noticed a single bud on a yellow daylily about to unfold. There is always one harbinger that springs up before the others, most of which won't really be in flower until the beginning of July. Also just about to bloom are the *Rosa rugosas* out along the water and on the road. The wild daisies, Oriental poppies, clematis, and most of the things in the perennial beds are getting ready, too.

Now is the time to cut out the ripened foliage from the daffodils. Some people wait until it really turns yellow before doing this, but I don't, and it doesn't seem to harm the bulbs. When the foliage starts lying on its side and flopping around, out it goes. If you have lots of bulbs, as I do, it is best to try to keep up with them as you go along. And, too, you want to give the plants around them room to breathe. I've also heard of braiding the leaves together while they are ripening, to make the beds look neater. I'm sure it does tidy things up, but sounds a bit baroque to me. Don't forget to give them bone meal after they have been cut.

This is a "fragrant" week in the garden and environs around me. Russian olive is everywhere—a good plant to know about if you live near the water and want a windbreak. They are in full flower now, and have an odor that always makes me think of summer to come. *Elaeagnus angustifolia* is the most prevalent species. It is considered a "second-rank" tree (small—to 20 feet). In addition to being able to withstand sea winds, it also doesn't seem too particular about other growing conditions, such as soil. It has silvery gray foliage, and the birds like its berries. Incidentally, I'm told it does well on city terraces. There is another species called thorny elaeagnus, which blooms in October and will add fragrance to the fall garden. Take a look at 'Aurea,' too, which has a leaf edged with yellow.

Also blooming now is wisteria. I've always been slightly ambivalent about this plant, wonderful childhood memories and its odor not withstanding. You must be very careful where you plant it, because it can do a great deal of damage to wooden structures. The trunk of the vine is very, very strong and can wreak havoc on shingles and gutters, and can even strangle special arbors made for it. I have one vine that has managed to work its way over to an electric pole. I'll probably be plunged into darkness one spring by its efforts. The best way to handle wisteria is to grow it away from the house, and prune the very daylights out of it after it blooms. There are some breathtakingly beautiful white varieties available these days.

Reminders

☐ Beginning this week, you should take the time to start edging all the beds with hand clippers. I have two pairs of electric ones with rechargeable batteries, which are among the best investments I ever made. It is amazing what a difference a nicely and neatly edged bed will make in the overall appearance of the garden.

☐ Don't forget to remove dead flowers from plants as they

bloom. This is not only healthy for the plants but also keeps the beds looking their best.

☐ Although you really should not transplant irises until about the third week of July, it is sometimes necessary to move them while they are in bloom, to be sure you are getting the right ones. After they have finished blooming, even if they have been marked, they can be difficult to locate, especially since the rhizomes tend to pile one on top of the other. Moving them now will stunt their growth, but sometimes it is the only way.

☐ Spray tent caterpillars, those unsightly nuisances you have probably begun to see indications of in the last few weeks. They can be stopped cold if sprayed at dusk—when they are back in their cozy tents after eating all your treasured plants. Any aerosol bomb meant to control bees and flying insects is good, because they usually have a long range. Keep an extra can of spray handy. Sometimes it is hard to spot the small infestations, and you should be ready when you do.

☐ If you have a big rainstorm, go out and cut the irises that won't be righted and remove any damaged flowers. Place them in a container of water and enjoy the flowers indoors. Depending on how mature the remaining buds are, they should all open. As the flowers fade indoors, pick them off. If they are allowed to stay on the stem and decompose, they will give up a juice the color of the iris, which can stain fabric.

'Love with Lace' iris is a midseason sturdy bloomer, despite its delicate name. In naming bearded iris and daylilies hybridizers seem to shed the Latin and burst into poetry . . . with mixed results. Hardy. Zones 4–9.

This thick perennial planting includes astilbe with its feathery white plumes, Centranthus or Jupiter's beard with its pink knobs, and a good yellow and white iris called 'Joyce Terry' combined with 'Dutch Chocolate.' Creeping over the rock in the foreground is one of the best little June bloomers—Geranium sanguineum prostratum (or just plain geranium)—a small, perfect plant with a long, difficult name! Zones 4–9.

All the parts of the flower of this iris, 'Prince Indigo,' are the same color, which gives it subtle drama. Be sure to include some of these dark blue purples in your garden. Zones 4–9.

This bouquet is made of irises that were knocked down by a storm. When this happens, I bring them into the house, where they will continue to bloom as long as I pick off dead flowers. Some of the varieties here are 'Love with Lace' (palest pink), 'West Coast' (hot yellow), 'Vermont' (white), and 'Cosmopolitan' (tan with lavender falls). All have been seen outside in some of the garden photographs. Zones 4–9.

Sometimes you can't have too much of a good thing. This planting of 'Pink Taffeta' irises follows masses of daffodils out by the driveway and is a welcome sight. Be certain that you really like the plants you choose for this sort of display. If you've any doubt, buy three or four different ones first to be sure. Zones 4–9.

This is a perennial planting that shows how important the various textures of leaves are in planning your garden. The dwarf Swiss pines (Pinus mugo) sunk into the deck give green form to the garden in spring and winter—and act as a foil in summer and fall for flowers. The spearlike leaves of both Siberian and bearded irises prevent monotony, and the bleeding heart (Dicentra) adds a softness. As bleeding heart dies back it will be followed by the tall self-seeding foxglove (Digitalis). Some of the bearded irises in bloom are 'Dutch Chocolate' (pale bronze), 'Normandie' (white and pale lavender), and 'Royal Trumpeter' (a rich maroon/bronze/red). These dark colors are wonderful in the bright light. Zones 4–9.

The tan iris with lavender falls is 'Cosmopolitan' and comes from Cooley's Gardens in Oregon. Their selections, along with those of Gilbert H. Wild and Son in Missouri, are dazzling. Many catalogs now include first-rate irises, so you can take your pick. Buying them in bloom from your garden center works all right if you are worried about color. Obviously, you can then see exactly what you are getting. The bronze iris is 'Spartan.' Zones 4–9.

This is my famous ten-year-old tulip. It comes up every year and blooms after all the others have gone, defying all the rules. It is the last of a group of bulbs brought to me from Holland, and by rights it should have run out years ago. I don't even know its name.

'Russel Hybrid' lupines

The Oriental poppy

'Festiva Maxima' peony

'Dresden Pink' peony

'Moon of Nippon' peony

Coreopsis and bicolored columbine

The Second Week of June

'Nelly Moser' clematis

Two colors of rhododendron

California poppies

The Second Week of June

This week was our first scorcher—heavy, still air and steady sun. I had to go into the city for several days just as the heat began, and when I returned I was absolutely amazed at the change that had come over the garden. Everything had decided to open at once! There seemed to be flowers everyplace you looked. Cream, peach, and light yellow irises in clumps along the drive. Dark brown, rust, purple, and multicolored irises combined with light lavender blue ones in the beds around the house. These had even been joined by bunches of chives, which got into the act with their clover-like flowers. And light pink Oriental poppies, which had been dawdling in full bud for over a week, followed suit. The beautiful bleeding hearts, which have been carrying so much of the burden of blossom for weeks, are continuing. Wild daisies and naturalized foxgloves are everywhere. (The big white foxgloves in the formal beds had opted to wait for another week.) In these wilder spots, along with the daisies and foxgloves, there are tall graceful grasses dotted with long-stemmed yellow Indian paintbrushes and white bladder campions. It takes only the slightest breeze (and they were slight this week) to set it all in soft waving motion—the sort of movement that is a joy to see through half-closed eyes. And the roses—practically tumbling off their trellises.

As marvelous as all this was to see, it made me realize how awfully tough these dramatic shifts in weather (remember the rainstorms and cool weather we had last week) can be on the unprepared garden. There are some things you can do, however, to take your garden through the season's extremes. At the beginning of the season, when ordering bulbs, check the height of tulips and irises. Shorter ones are better, because they are less likely to snap. With things like peonies you have no real choice except staking. All plants look better in groups, and this is an additional safeguard. Arrange your most vulnerable double tulips (or any other damage-prone variety) in a group that can be lifted right out of the garden if disaster strikes. A plant from the garden center can fill any empty place. This isn't cheating. The venerable Gertrude Jekyll was known to slip in a spare plant from the "nursery bed," and gardener and writer Christopher Lloyd advises good gardeners to have duplicates waiting in the wings.

Don't overfertilize; it's almost better to use too little than too much. Extra fertilizer encourages extra growth and leads to floppiness.

Stake early. There are some plants that almost must be staked if you want to grow them successfully. If you don't want the bother, don't grow the plant.

After a severe rainstorm, if your garden is ravaged, be prepared for extreme surgery. Be tough. Cut back hard any seriously damaged plants—they'll doubtless revive before the season is too far along. Remember how quickly plants grow this time of the year; the word *perennial* means just that. Add fertilizer, but not too much, and wait for a rebloom in the fall or next year. It's the thought of next year that keeps really good gardeners going.

Summer drought, the opposite weather extreme, is the gardener's bane and the beach-goer's joy. It's also hard on gardens. But you can have it both ways. Automatic timers and built-in irrigation have taken a lot of the sting out of this part of gardening. Watering was always something I didn't like doing. But it is not just water alone that is needed. Many plants want cool nights to revive, as well as a bit of natural rain to wash dust off their leaves. There are techniques to help here too. However, the starting point of any gardening technique is "awareness"—awareness of the needs of your plants, as well as, and balanced against, your own needs. Remember what I said in my introduction about the size of your garden. Be honest about how large a one you can keep in good order by yourself. Even if you have someone to help you, there will still be times when you will be on your own—and think about the time you want to spend playing tennis or fishing or going to the beach or attending to the needs of your children. If you rent out your house for a part of the season, don't expect anything from your tenants. They didn't pay their money to think about your garden.

Most garden encyclopedias have sections on dry gardening. Some of the best flowers listed there don't necessarily make pretty bouquets but are good steady growers. Sedums of every kind. Euphorbias and yuccas are extreme examples, but yarrows, anthemis (yellow chamomile) and butterfly weeds, asters, coreopsis, pinks, sunflowers, and all their cousins are hardy and pretty. Or statice and rudbeckia. All can take the heat.

Install the watering system early in the spring if you are going to do it, because it's hard on plants later on. Soaker hoses can be snaked through the garden and hidden by growing leaves. Automatic timers will do the rest. And water deeply. Shallow watering isn't worth a damn; it only encourages shallow roots, which dry out twice as fast. A good rule of thumb is an inch of water a week, either natural or applied. An inexpensive rain gauge is handy. Try to water in the early morning or late afternoon. Roses don't particularly want their leaves wet, because they can get black spot, which is caused by a fungus, but almost everything else does.

Mulching really helps. Use compost, if you have it, with an icing of salt hay, thinly spread over any bare ground. Don't make this mulch too dense, or it will become a haven for pests. Peat moss is a mixed blessing, because if it dries out, it's like a raincoat and literally sheds the water. Cultivate shallowly and remove weeds, which compete for nutrients with good plants. Don't let the dirt get hard like cement. You avoid this by improving the soil with a rough-textured filler. Other good mulches are finely shredded bark, cocoa hulls, and, for plants that do well in acid soil, pine needles, which are my favorite.

Deadhead regularly, and fertilize lightly after watering, not before. If you keep cool yourself, and stick to your routine, your plants will respond with a good show of flowers when cooler weather arrives. Fall is a lovely season and a rewarding one—but aren't they all?

Don't try to sow grass seeds or set out seedlings in the heat. If you must put out small plants, be prepared to give them plenty of attention—water and shade.

These Lupinus regalis, *Russel strain, in mixed colors really do best in a cool climate. For that reason, they should be rather heavily mulched to insulate their roots when the weather gets hot. And they must have water when it gets dry. They are long-lasting flowers, excellent for cutting, and come in a very wide range of colors. Hardy in Zones 4–7.*

This, the commonest of the white peonies, Paeonia lactiflora *'Festiva Maxima,' is also one of the prettiest. All peonies want to be heavily fed in late winter or early spring. These big bloomers really need to be staked so that their heads don't bend over and break in spring rainstorms. Place three sturdy stakes (½ inch in diameter and 3 feet tall) in a triangle around the plant when leaves are about 8 to 10 inches high, and wind twistems around them as the plant grows. Try to disguise the stakes by leaving some of the foliage outside the twistems so that they are less visible. Zones 3–8.*

This single white Japanese peony is called 'Moon of Nippon' and can withstand wild spring weather. It also has elegant foliage, but when you pick the flowers, don't take too many leaves, as the plant needs them for its health. Give peonies plenty of room when you plant them—at least 3 feet. They don't much want to be moved, so settle them in thoughtfully. Zones 3–8.

Oriental poppies, Papaver orientale, *are not grown by some gardeners because their blooming period is so brief. But I think they are worth it. So did Monet, who had them planted abundantly at Giverny. They like sun, and if you grow them mark the spot with a stake so you won't disturb the clump after it goes dormant. Since they are taprooted, you can slip a few annuals over them. They make an excellent cut flower if you pick them just as the bud is opening and burn the stems before putting them in water. This one is 'Mrs. Perry.' Zone 2 and southward.*

This is a beautiful double pink peony, Paeonia lactiflora *'Dresden Pink.' Its growing habits are the same as for the other peonies mentioned here. Zones 3–8.*

Two old-fashioned favorites—tickseed, or coreopsis, and columbine (Aquilegia). The yellow coreopsis is almost a weed and blooms off and on all summer, with its peak in late June and July. The cultivated form, C. grandiflora 'Sunray,' is shown here. Hardy in Zones 3–9.

Clematis likes to have its feet cool and its branches in the sun. It also wants water when the weather gets exceptionally hot—and a shovelful of manure and/or compost at its base in November. 'Nelly Moser,' which you see here, is a nonstop bloomer during its season. It can stand winter in Zone 3 and needs only to be securely tied so that its brittle branches don't break when it is windy.

Unlike some members of the poppy family, these California poppies (Eschscholzia) do not need to have their stems sealed over a flame when they are picked. They last surprisingly well in the house, but close at night.

Rhododendrons are useful plants in the garden, providing privacy and form for the landscape. Their shiny foliage does best with some slight protection from the sun. And since they are shallow-rooted, they really need a mulch around their base. Water if it's extremely dry. When buying plants, check on flower color. Many are pastels, but there are now bright reds and sharp purples on the market. Make sure your plants are harmonious together. Their colors can present the same problems as azaleas. Zones 5–8.

Siberian iris and sage blossoms

Purple Siberian iris

Iceland poppies

Bleeding heart and Siberian iris blooming in the perennial bed

The Third Week of June

Viburnum and bridal wreath

White foxglove, Siberian iris, and wild daisies in a garden bed

Siberian iris, chive blossoms, and wild daisies

The Third Week of June

We have a pause in the iris parade this week, with just a few last flowers left of the bearded and Siberians. There are lots of buds on the Japanese irises, but it looks as though blooms are still a week or so away.

In the meantime, the great majestic spikes of white foxglove in the beds closest to the house have opened. I've been growing them for so many years that I had forgotten how I got around to them in the first place—until I saw some beautiful delphiniums a few days ago. It isn't cold enough in Louisiana for delphiniums, so we had to do with the smaller-scale annual larkspur instead. I still have a weakness for larkspur, and grow it every few years. However, when I first started gardening in Bridgehampton I couldn't wait to try my hand at delphiniums. Each attempt ended in dismal failure. They were forever rotting or getting blown over. In the second year they would send up a pathetic little spire that was a travesty of the splendid original, and then die. Salt air, strong winds, and sandy soil are just a combination that they couldn't bear. Then one year I planted big white foxgloves in the spot where I had wanted the delphiniums. They are tough plants and a perfect substitute—although I no longer think of them as a substitute. They are grand flowers in their own right. They also have an interesting growing pattern, which I like. The mother plant gets larger and larger for several years and then suddenly begins to disappear, leaving her space blank—in the meantime having sent up new plants in her vicinity. This process forces me to change the arrangement of the perennial bed, keeping it always in a state of flux. The first time this happened, I went to my nurseryman to buy a new plant. He asked me if I hadn't bought some from him three or four years back. When I said yes, but one had died, he told me to go back and look around. Of course, I did, and found many young ones to transplant. That is what I've been doing ever since.

Daisies are still everyplace. Remembering my experience with foxgloves reminds me of how I got the daisies started here. They seemed to grow in great abundance all over—but there were none on my property. The first year, after they matured along the road

I collected an enormous bucket of seeds and sprinkled them around in the fall, my head filled with visions of great sweeps of them come spring. To my dismay, the next year I had only a few measly plants. But I was undaunted. When I collected seeds this time, I cut off the dry heads and left the whole head of seeds intact. These were strewn around, and the following year I got my wish. Incidentally, did you know that *daisy* means "day's eye"? (Something for you to throw in when there is a lull in the cocktail conversation.)

As it has gotten warmer and more humid, I have had a few more infestations of aphids on the roses' new growth. I've kept control by just spraying them off with a jet of water. If things get serious for you, use insecticidal soap. This should not be applied in strong sunlight or you will run the risk of burning the plant. Do it in the evening or early morning, and several hours later spray off the residue with plain water.

After a hot spell, beware of buying bedding plants or potted perennials. In garden centers the heat comes up from under the plant containers and damages them pretty badly. If a plant or tray of seedlings seems limp or slightly wilted, think twice before investing in it. Even if they grow, you might have to overcome the shock they have been put through. However, this might be a secondhand blessing if you are short of budget and an attentive gardener, because you can sometimes get these heat-stricken plants at bargain prices. Wilted foliage can be trimmed and you can get them going. It will take longer, and they won't look exactly terrific for the first couple of weeks, but this is a way to stretch the gardening money. Don't ever do this with trees or shrubs. Centers usually don't guarantee these, and you might get stuck.

This is a good time to start pruning your early-blooming shrubs—the ones that have already finished for the season, such as forsythia and lilac (and some azaleas). Rhododendrons still have a few more weeks to go, so you can get at them later. Cut out about a third of the old lilac and forsythia branches at the base if the plant has become overgrown. When pruning, try to reinforce the natural structure of the plant. Do not try to make it into a formal shape, which invariably produces hideous results. There is a very good reason for pruning these particular shrubs at this time of the year. By fall they have already begun to set their buds for the following spring, and you would be getting rid of next year's flowers if they were pruned late in the season. When you get around to the rhododendrons, be very careful not to cut off the new growth, which lies just beside the spent flowers. All plants benefit from a good circulation of air, so if shrubs are dense, cut some wood out of their centers.

Speaking of shrubs, this is also a good time to plant some varieties. One of the prettiest is one commonly called beauty bush *(Kolkwitzia amabilis)*. It makes a great fountain of pale pink flowers for about three weeks this month, so when you buy it you will likely be able to see what the flowers look like. These are similar to the old favorite *Weigela*, but I think nicer. It has few requirements and can stand some dryness and cold winters (Zones 4–8). At maturity it stands about 8 feet.

If you need a dwarf shrub, one of the toughest around is Wayside's cinquefoil, or just plain buttercup shrub. It is so hardy that it grows from Zone 2 to Zone 7, which means it can take temperatures of from minus fifty degrees up to heat in the nineties in the summer. There is even a good color range—from white to yellow to a kind of reddish orange. I think you will find 'Gold Star' one of the best yellows. 'Abbotswood' has bluish foliage and white flowers. The full-grown bush is about 30 inches across and blooms from June into the middle of July, throwing out flowers at random after that.

Another dwarf of good quality is the late-blooming lilac from Korea called *Syringa* 'Miss Kim.' It has fragrant single flowers for about three weeks and is hardy from Zone 3 through Zone 8—so you know it is a pretty tough bird too.

You see a lot of ground cover in the garden centers this time of the year. And, of course, there are times and conditions when it works where nothing else will. Of all of them I think I prefer the old myrtle with its unassuming little purple flowers. Pachysandra always does well, but it has been used so much commercially that I am a bit tired of it—but it *is* dependable. Another old favorite is Star-of-David, which has marvelously fragrant white blossoms. If it isn't controlled, it can invade the lawn and become a bit of a nuisance. One of the worst offenders in terms of taking over where you don't want it is *Ajuga*, also called bugle. It can really become a pest. The bronze-leaf variety can look quite gloomy in the lawn, too. Beware.

There is a variety of viburnum in bloom now that is quite common called Japanese snowball. Some people don't like it because it is so ordinary, but left out in an open area it makes a very nice show and always makes me know summer is here.

Siberian irises (Iris sibirica) *are different from bearded in that the bearded types prefer a drier, relatively acid-free soil and Siberians the opposite. Both grow happily together in this garden, but that is partly because the garden is somewhat on the dry side. Siberian irises are excellent for naturalizing and blurring the edges between the very domestic part of the landscape and the wilder areas beyond the lawn. This variety is* 'Caesar's Brother' *and is mixed with lavender garden sage blossoms* (Salvia). *Zones 4–9.*

Poppies are among my favorite cut flowers, and Iceland poppies (Papaver nudicaule) *are perennials that will grow in the South but like cold weather. Mine tend to die out after several years—a few at a time. When the flowers are cut, the ends of their stems should be singed over an open flame to seal them. Aside from their beautiful tissuelike petals, I am particularly fond of their eccentric stems. For best results Zones 1–5.*

A very hardy strain of Siberian iris, I. sibirica 'Flight of Butterflies.' *It makes such a thick mat of roots that you have to be careful where you plant it. Be sure it has room to spread. Zones 4–9.*

This is an older planting of Siberian iris (Iris sibirica) *grown with several varieties of bleeding heart* (Dicentra) *and foxglove* (Digitalis) *about to bloom.*

The long-necked laboratory boiling flask is one of my favorite flower holders. It is particularly useful for showing off branches with long stems, because the narrow neck holds them in place. Old-time shrubs you see here are Vibernum opulus 'Sterile' *and bridal wreath* (Spiraea). *They will grow anywhere, being hardy in Zones 3–8. Bridal wreath, despite its name, is not very pretty when not in bloom, so I wouldn't recommend buying it.*

The colors of 'Flight of Butterflies' *Siberian iris and chive blossoms are particularly nice together. Here, they are joined in a bouquet by wild daisies* (Chrysanthemum leucanthemum), *peas* (Pisum sativum), *and grass.*

White foxglove in a bed, with white Siberian iris and wild daisies in the foreground.

Pink 'Inspiration' roses and white Rosa rugosa

'Maiden's Blush' roses

'Ivory Fashion' rose

A glorious rose, 'Medallion'

A pristine pink rose with a selection of ivory roses

A selection of June roses

The Last Week of June

The Last Week of June

I forgot to mention last week that one of my favorite flowers has opened in the garden. It is the Iceland poppy. As a matter of fact, I am a sucker for all members of the poppy family. Their petals are a marvel of bright color—the only flowers which are so bright that I like. The Iceland poppy is a perennial and will last in the garden for a number of years. Its blossoms are yellow, orange, and white, with an occasional pinkish red thrown in. They are in bloom longer than their big showy cousin, the Oriental poppy, which is now available in a tremendous range of interesting colors instead of the Halloween orange and black that is around everyplace. There is another cousin, an annual, called the Shirley poppy. Their single flowers (doubles too) bloom in a gorgeous range of pinks, reds, and lavenders, as well as more neutral tones, and their petals are often crinkled. I am forever trying to grow this strain, and sometimes it works spectacularly; at others I get nothing at all. If you replant them in the same bed year after year, you will get quite a few volunteers. Their seeds are extremely fine, which can make it rather hard to keep them from bunching up when they are planted. To get around this, you can mix them with fine sand before they are broadcast onto the prepared bed. They germinate while the weather is still cold, so should be planted in the fall and covered with a thin layer of hay. Be on the lookout for signs of slugs when seeds start to grow, because these pests can decimate a patch of young seedlings practically overnight. If you don't have any luck with your fall planting, you still have a chance at a second planting if you get to it at the beginning of April. Although the flowers look fragile, the plants, once established, are really tough. They also make lovely cut flowers with their eccentrically shaped stems and translucent petals. It doesn't take many to make a statement.

A few of the Japanese irises have opened this week. Ditto the daylilies. Both will probably flood me with flowers next week.

All this month there are many varieties of wildflowers in bloom in the meadows and along the roads—and of course in the woods. Once you start noticing them, you will be amazed to discover how many there are around. Incidentally, on the bargain tables of bookstores or book departments you will many times find books on wildflowers with good color photographs. These can enhance your pleasure as you begin to know them by name. I've never tried to get any wildflowers going here from seed except daisies. (I don't count the poppies, wild geraniums, and trilliums under the bayberry, because they were transplants.) I'm constantly astounded by what pops up that I never saw (or noticed) before. I have bladder campion, Japanese honeysuckle, white sweet clover, red clover, soapwort, white yarrow, pokeweed, dock, bugleweed, daisy fleabane, meadow rue, Queen Anne's lace, winter cress, hawkweed, buttercup, black-eyed Susan, wild sweet pea, tansy, butter-and-eggs, king-devil, blazing star, vetch, blue vervain, thistle, flax, gerardia, chicory, wild aster, and all kinds of goldenrod, plus others I don't know the names of. And several wild roses.

By now you should have a pretty good idea of what state your perennials are in. Some undoubtedly have begun to run out or just didn't make it through the winter. Others might be beginning to crowd things too much. And then there will be holes and blanks to be filled in. This is about your last good chance to get annuals, provided they are still fresh. Among those that are useful are petunias, which often are available in fairly big pots, because they will sprawl out in a fairly short time and give you a nice mass of bloom—and will continue to flower so long as you keep them deadheaded. There is a very wide range of color in the family, too. Don't forget one of my other favorites: verbena.

You are apt to still see some cosmos around, as well as cleomes and nicotianas, to give you a bit of height. Speaking of nicotianas, if you have a sunny window facing east or vaguely northeast, they will grow nicely in the house. The trick is to put them where they will not have to be moved—and ideally on a tray of gravel, so that watering will not be a chore—placing several pots close together so they will support one another. I did this one year, and by pinching off the flower stems when they bloomed out to the end, I got flowers until fall, and they didn't get too leggy until almost the end. Because of the lack of air circulation, they are susceptible to bugs, so keep them inspected and give them a spraying at the first sign of trouble.

Periwinkle is a cheerful little plant that can be useful now; it has flowers like myrtle, and is also available in white and pink. Unlike myrtle, it is not a vine. White Shasta daisies are a good balance in a colorful border, and especially good next to something like the orange 'Enchantment' lilies. On the other hand, if you want a touch of yellow or orange with yellow, there is coreopsis (which naturalizes when it escapes out into the wild) or gaillardia. Both of these are perennial.

Purple coneflower or rudbeckia will create a strong patch of color, which can be diluted with another one of my favorites, also perennial, false dragonhead. It is usually seen in pinks but comes in white. All sorts of astilbe are around now, and many other varieties of perennials that seem to be members of the thistle family (without the prickles). The advantage of buying these blooming perennials is that you know exactly what you are getting, and you also get instant results. Also, by buying plants in bloom you can see how the colors go together. You can shift things around a little later on if you take the time to make some notes now. Or, if you are willing to be very careful and do transplanting on a cool day *and* be generous with the daily watering until they get over the shock of moving, you can move a few anytime.

Reminders

☐ Keep watering. If the garden is dry you really must keep at it. This is especially true of plants that are coming into bloom, which will benefit from the extra boost to counteract summer evaporation. A task with less immediate results is to keep ferns and other moisture-loving plants, such as primulas, damp. You'll be repaid by better flowers next spring. (I know it is sometimes difficult to keep such long-range rewards in mind.) During a very dry spell, it is best to divide your garden into areas and give a different area a good deep soaking each day in addition to the general watering you do. This is also a time to be extremely attentive to newly planted trees and shrubs. A properly planted tree (or shrub) usually has a little well around it, which holds the water until it soaks in. This first year is crucial, and they must never be allowed to dry out when the weather is uncooperative. The killer of most new plantings is lack of water. Remember what I said earlier about deep watering or soaking: it encourages deep roots, which are best. The only thing that is in most gardens that doesn't seem to mind these rainless periods is the bearded iris.

☐ Keep staking the dahlias, and watch out for loosened ties after you get that big rainstorm.

☐ Keep fertilizing the roses every few weeks while they are blooming, and be on the lookout for those aphids and mites.

'Inspiration' is a very hardy climbing rose that blooms continually all summer if you keep the dead heads cut off. It makes strong canes, and the flowers are held on extremely long and sturdy stems. *Rosa rugosa* is a naturalized rose that grows down by the water.

The beautiful and hardy 'Ivory Fashion' rose. Its startling orangy yellow center is surrounded by deep ivory petals.

This magnificent rose is called 'Medallion.' It has a lovely scent and makes perfect flowers held on sturdy stems.

This group of roses contains a Portland rose called 'Rose du Roi' (dark bluish red in the center of the photograph). This rose is over 150 years old and an important forerunner of today's Hybrid Perpetuals. The pinks are 'Inspiration' on the left and 'Climbing La France' on the right. The bright red at the top is another old Hybrid Perpetual called 'General Jacqueminot.' It flowers repeatedly.

This multipetaled rose is *Rosa alba incarnata* 'Great Maiden's Blush.' The color is beautiful and it has a wonderful fragrance. Its foliage is a blue green. It grows to a height of 4 to 6 feet.

The pink rose is called 'Queen Elizabeth.' The ivory and white garden roses are from Roses of Yesteryear.

Roses thrive in almost every climate, and some are hardier than others. Here is a selection of different varieties, some older (from Roses of Yesteryear) and some more contemporary. Usually the company you're ordering from will give you specific instructions for growing.

How to Make Potpourri

How to Make Potpourri

I suspect that when you mention potpourri to most people, they think of roses. And when the air is full of the scent of roses, I always think how nice if it could be that way all the time. Potpourri lets you have at least an echo of this pleasure during the winter.

Many of the more hybridized roses, as well as some wild varieties, don't have enough odor to use, but since I am partial to the older roses, which usually throw out a wonderful fragrance, this is no problem. Too, many of these have what seem like hundreds of petals in each blossom.

There are two basic methods for making this summer-scented mixture: dry and wet. The dry method utilizes petals that are dried before they are used. This process, though simple, must be carefully done with small quantities so that the petals will not mildew before they give up their moisture. This can require a good amount of space if you want to do a large batch at one time. An old shed or studio where the flower petals on their trays would not have to be moved much would be perfect. I don't have such a space (or the temperament), so it is the wet method for me. And that is the one I'll be telling you about here. If you want to know more about the dry method, I suggest you stop at your local library, because there are often sections on potpourri in some of the older gardening books.

I hate to tell you, but this is another one of those things you learn by doing. It is best to just start, because the basic technique is extremely easy and a snap to master. The part that requires your personal touch (and your experience of doing it) is the combination of scents—petals, spices, and citrus—you put together to come up with something that smells right to you. For me this is like buying a tie; no one else can really do it for me. The first try you will probably be contented with the roses alone, which should be the basis for what you devise anyway. You might want to experiment with a number of smaller batches in order to become acquainted with possible combinations. One problem to be aware of is the comparative delicacy of some scents. You should learn

Overleaf: *Roses, verbena, honeysuckle, mint, chervil, thyme, and tuberoses gathered for potpourri*

how to balance one with another. Don't let that put you off; you can do it. After all, you know when something smells good to you—and that is the point.

You will need a large opaque crock or earthenware container with a good tight lid. Make sure it is clean and dry. In this you put a layer of rose petals about an inch deep. Sprinkle it with a thin coating of salt (preferably kosher). Make a number of layers, and as they begin to settle down as days pass, top with new layers (with salt), each time giving it all a stir first. By fall you have a crockful of petals ready for use.

Many other things may be added to this basic ingredient: honeysuckle, mock orange, lemon verbena, and azalea, to name a few. But the one that offers the greatest variety is the scented-leaved geranium; they smell of orange, lemon, pineapple, verbena, mint, and things in between. In the case of the geranium, you use the leaf, not the flowers. And until you come up with a combination that you know will work for you, it is probably best to dry these things in separate crocks. Later you can do it all at once and correct the balance with a few spices.

You may also use the leaves of herbs like thyme, rosemary, and marjoram, as well as spices such as ground cloves and allspice.

One of my favorite additions is the dried skin of orange or lemon. The citrus and spices are added to the final mix, not as you go along. To prepare citrus, peel fruit and set out the rind on a surface that allows good air circulation (a piece of coarse screen or netting). Turn the rind every few days to prevent mildew. Let it rest in a cool place until dry.

Care must be taken when you gather the petals. Ideally this is done when they are dry, so it should not be in the morning, as with cut flowers. The oil that you are after is released when the petals are crushed and is concentrated, in the case of roses, at the base of the petal. So select roses that are at their peak of maturity and snip the heads—then pull petals off gently. If you carry a small basket with you, you can hold it under the flowers and let them fall in as you cut. The less you handle them the better.

When gathering herbs or the leaves of geraniums, the same advice applies: snip them off. Do not try to pull or pinch leaves. They don't want to be crushed.

To make your final combination, start with a proportionately large quantity of rose petals, to which you add a bit of dried orange or lemon rind and then a pinch of cloves or allspice. This is the simplest combination. When you have a feel for it, try using some of the other herbs and flowers you have prepared.

As you can imagine, there is no real recipe for this, because the intensity of the odors would vary with each batch of leaves and petals. But your nose knows. There are recipes in books like the very good one on herbs from the Time-Life series, but these should be used only as guides. Don't be afraid to change the proportions if the outcome doesn't suit you.

Keep your finished stash of potpourri in a tightly covered container until you are ready to use it. There are traditional boxes and jars made of china or wood for potpourri. These generally have perforated tops to allow the scent to escape. These tops serve a dual purpose, keeping the dust out while the room is perfumed. Baskets can be used, but since they are porous it is best to line them with a bit of foil to keep the odor trapped and so that bits of the dried ingredients won't sift out onto the table. Some people merely put potpourri in a jar with a top and remove the top when they want to enjoy the scent. Warmth seems to activate the oils that produce fragrance. The whole batch should be given a gentle stirring when it is opened. It will lose its potency after a time, but a good batch will see you through the bleakest part of the winter, until you can start over again.

Just remember, the name of the game is "experiment." This is the only way you will get the kind of results that are personal and suit you best. Of course, potpourri makes a marvelous and welcome gift—if you can part with any.

JULY

Overleaf: *The nation celebrates its birthday . . . and the daylilies celebrate too*

JULY

For a sizable segment of the population, July is synonymous with summer. To middle-aged folk it often conjures up images of picnics and fireworks in a nostalgically recalled childhood that probably never really was. For a younger generation, it is likely the image of other teenagers horsing around in or with water. (With a freezer of iced drinks somewhere in the foreground.)

I guess I am in the former group, although where I grew up there wasn't much in the way of fireworks. But what July means to me now that I have gotten the gardening bug (no pun) is lilies and annuals in bloom. Daylilies, tough old orange tiger lilies, hybrids, snapdragons, calendulas, larkspurs, and cleomes—and, oddly enough, the appealing imperfections of field- and yard-grown flowers. The other day I was struck by how much charm bouquets made with these natural blossoms have. An "arrangement" made up of beautiful, perfect, and somewhat exotic specimens tastefully selected was sent to me from a local florist. It was very pretty, but too perfect. In fact, it looked so odd in my house that I finally took it all apart. I felt a bit guilty doing this, and thought about it several times during the day. The problem was that this commercially prepared bouquet called attention to itself, and in the wrong way. A big handful of wild daisies stuck into a pitcher or a single blossom held aloft on an oddly shaped stem are right at home. An arrangement of the sort sent to me almost seems an end in itself, while an unselfconscious bouquet is just a member of the family. Maybe I'm making too much of this (my guilt at taking the thoughtful arrangement apart?). Certainly, there is a place for meticulously arranged flowers—in a bank lobby perhaps—but that place just isn't my house.

This month is when gardening settles down to what some refer to as weeding and watering time. It surely is when all the weeding and watering produce results. Also, it is the month when emphasis shifts around in the garden, from a part that has been blooming continuously for the last months to another area that has just started. It is also when annuals really begin making their appearance. Big hybrid daisies and glamorized versions of the plain black-eyed Susans. Followed by stocks, zinnias, cleomes, snapdragons, and on and on.

This change also produces a change in the kind of bouquets I start putting around. Instead of depending on great quantities of one kind of flower in many variations, bouquets become more mixed. There is so much to choose from, and it is different from week to week.

While the flower beds are in transition this month and the annuals planted to fill the gaps are getting settled in, it is particularly important to keep these beds pruned and well mulched. This neat and manicured appearance will help to emphasize the flowers that are still in bloom. It also is important to keep these beds properly edged. Grass grows very quickly this time of the year, especially if you are a serious waterer.

Of course, predicting is always risky, particularly about the weather. But in July we start getting those long hot days and the pattern becomes more stable—if it is going to. This is a time to sit and appreciate your handiwork. For me it is a time to roll out of bed early enough to see the sun come up over the pond and fill the garden. A time for all the windows to be open, and to pad around with bare feet. A time not to think of how close we will be to fall at the end of the month. For a brief now all there is is summer.

The First Week of July

Two kinds of daylilies

The First Week of July

The Japanese irises spotted around in the beds and the daylilies on the bank have more than fulfilled their promise of last week. Irises have been opening in waves during the past seven days—gorgeous dark purple with markings of bright yellow, blue-veined whites, and pinkish lavenders all set against great masses of white irises, astilbes, foxgloves, and wild daisies, which are still blooming away. I realize more than ever the importance of all this white I have planted everyplace. It is a formula I've always been partial to in design projects—and not just gardening ones. With white (against green), vivid colors absolutely pop out, while subtle shades can easily be seen and appreciated. At the other end of the spectrum, dark reds and purples, which almost blend in with weathered wood, are equally beautiful. But then, so is light pink.

On the embankment in front of the house, the two colors of daylilies have gotten going. I can always count on them to be in full glory by the fourth of July. When the house was first built, I started out with the common orange variety that you see growing everywhere—which a farmer let me dig up from his field. About ten years ago, I added a very good strain of bright yellow lilies that my aunt sent me from Natchez. She didn't know the name, but they were obviously a very old variety and are unbelievably hardy—coming into bloom about a week after the orange ones. I learned something interesting about daylilies having to do with that garden pest the rabbit (I am cursed with many of them). For some reason known only to rabbits, they don't much care for daylily foliage, so I am able to plant other kinds of lilies (which bunnies love) in with them on the bank. And either they go unnoticed or the rabbits don't want to wade through the unsavory daylilies to get to them. Rabbits will also leave narcissus, bearded irises, foxgloves, and violas alone.

The darker daylilies along the drive are in bud, with just a few showing color. These will be coming into flower in a few weeks, overlapping slightly with those on the embankment. After their big show, they will continue to throw out a flower or two until fall.

This week I bought a flat of white periwinkles with a spot of dark pink for an eye. I've scattered them around in the beds to fill in when many of the perennials have completed their cycle. I haven't thought of, or planted, them in years, but when I saw these I was reminded of how much my grandmother had liked them. Maybe having written about her recently in the introduction to this book made me want to remember her when I look at the garden. Oddly enough, my garden looks nothing like hers.

I also found that a few pink snapdragons had reseeded themselves around where there had been several plants last year. These were a pleasant surprise, and I moved them out so they would have more room. I never stake my snapdragons if I can help it. I'd rather let those that want to, fall over. Then all the secondary stems will shoot straight up and flower, making a good mass of color.

The lilies in the fenced-in cutting garden out back are in bud and should be opening this coming week. I planted a white variety called 'Black Dragon.' I'm very partial to the odor of lilies. When you cut only one stem and bring it in, it fills the room with a marvelous fragrance. They are especially nice on a night table.

I'm letting the foxgloves in the wild garden go to seed. I'll harvest them in August and broadcast them around to get a denser show of flowers next spring. I've noticed that about now each year—right in the midst of all the riotous flowering—I begin to think seriously about next year.

I have also discovered a clump of white foxgloves in bloom on a bank down by the water. The birds must have dropped a seed there. I've put a marker by the plant so that when it finishes blooming, it can be moved into one of the front beds with the other whites.

My hostas are in bloom. The only variety I have is named 'Eleganta' and is a bright white (naturally) with lush foliage. *Hosta* is a very large genus of plants, and many people grow dozens of varieties. The foliage is often more interesting than the flowers, being both bicolor and solid. Frankly, I've never gotten on to them that much. Incidentally, they are also called plantain lily. If you like them, different varieties will let you have blooms from spring right through fall.

Reminders

☐ To rejuvenate annuals that have become tall and skinny, cut them back hard and give them a shot of 5-10-5 fertilizer every two weeks. This will get them going again with new growth and new flowers.

☐ Keep watering if it doesn't rain. Don't worry if plants look wilted or limp on a hot afternoon; they'll revive when it turns cooler in the evening and they have a chance to take in some water.

☐ Keep an eye out for plants that have become overly dense. These should be thinned out so they will get good air circulation, which helps to keep them disease-free and fungus-clean. When you deadhead flowers, put the picked heads into a bucket and discard. Do not throw them on the mulch, as decomposing petals give pests a place to hide and thrive. The observant gardener will spot problems—like a speck of black spot on a rose leaf, which can be picked, or slugs napping at the base of some prized tender plant (which can be dropped into a glass of beer). This emphasis on prevention allows the gardener to use few sprays and poisons—as you may recall my pointing out earlier, it is sometimes enough to wash away a few aphids with a spray of water. You can live with a few bugs and save the heavy ammunition for serious matters.

☐ Keep weeding (of course). One of the handiest tools is the hand "claw" cultivator. Narrow ones are best, because they allow you to get between the plants without pulling them up by the roots. If you use the short-handled one you'll be closer to your plants and can observe better what is going on, but a long-handled one is easier on the back.

☐ If you are not a full-season gardener, but have just rented a house for a few months' vacation, take advantage of the summer sales many garden centers have about now. Annuals are cheap, provide quick color, and require just a touch of horticultural skill. Pamper them and you will have them blooming in several weeks. Don't make the mistake of trying to set yourself up with a full-scale flower bed, however; it is too late for that. Tuck plants where you'll see them when you are having your morning coffee or taking an outdoor shower when you come back from the beach—or in a tub by the front or kitchen door. If your time is really limited, geraniums are the answer. Just don't overwater or overfertilize them, and keep the dead leaves and flowers picked off.

☐ You might also want to consider a child's garden if you have young ones with you. Make the garden small, about a yard square—a realistic size. Try scarlet runner beans, which can be trained on a teepee of 6-foot poles—you will have to finish off the tops. Soak seeds overnight for faster germination. You probably won't get any beans, but you will get lots of growth. 'Tom Thumb' tomatoes can still be bought as started plants. Add to this a six-pack of small marigolds or zinnias for a bit of color. And always allow children to exercise their own taste (which probably won't suit yours). Just put the bed where you don't have to look at it. The aim is to have fun.

These tiger lilies (Lilium lancifolium splendens) are very tough and are perfect for naturalizing, because they spread rapidly. They reach a height of 4 feet or more and have very strong stems.

Daylilies (Hemerocallis) are not the best cut flowers, because each flower lasts only a single day. Stems must be picked with mature buds, which will keep opening over a period of several days. Seen here is 'King of Hearts' on the right and the rarer (and more expensive) 'Cross my Heart.' Zones 3–10.

Yarrow, sea lavender, and feverfew

'Sterling Star' lilies

Japanese iris, baby's breath, and Shasta daisies

Cleomes, snapdragons, and zinnias

The Second Week of July

The Second Week of July

Buds on the white foxglove have opened up to the very top. My sometime garden helper and I have been cutting flowers off down below as they die, but the plants themselves are beginning to take on a yellowish cast, telling us their season is almost done. The same thing is happening to the old-fashioned bleeding hearts. And the white ones as well. All will have to be cut back.

I imagine before next week is half finished the Japanese irises, which have made such a spectacular showing this year, will be through except for a few stragglers. During their blooming period we have kept the spent flower heads snipped off. This not only makes the beds neater, but helps to keep stems from being weighted down, which is especially important when we have strong wind and rain. If stems are not top-heavy, when the sun comes out they will spring right back up and dry off. It is a good idea to be on the lookout for snails and slugs in your iris beds, too—they go right up the stems to get at the tender flowers. They seem to be particularly partial to my Japanese irises.

Wild daisies are beginning to look a bit ragged. This week we start working on them—clipping them off at the ground. With all this cutting and pruning, for the next few weeks the beds will look somewhat sparse before the bedding plants become established. Some of the bedding plants will have to be moved in where we have cut out foliage. Fortunately, we still have veronicas and astilbes blooming, and the snapdragons are all out. Cosmos will also continue for a while yet.

This time of the summer, when there is a pause of several weeks while the beds come back into flower, the emphasis shifts away from the house to the great display of daylilies along the drive and on the bank.

Hybridizers have been working overtime developing new strains of daylilies. The color range now is exceedingly wide and includes pinks as well as whites. These are extremely tough plants and thrive in Zones 3–10. Everyone recommends these for lazy gardeners, and they are right. Plants will bloom for years without dividing. As a matter of fact, the ones on the bank have *never* been divided. They would probably be the better for

it, but I can't face the chore. Anyway, they are unfussy, but need the usual pampering the first year—as any other plant does. Remember what I said earlier about planting daffodils in with these, because the daylily foliage comes in just in time to hide the maturing daffodil foliage, cutting down on your manicuring.

Among the most satisfactory are 'Hyperion,' a clear yellow that has been around for over fifty years, and 'Mary Todd,' a hot gold tetraploid. Tetraploid refers to, in this case, the double number of petals carried in the blossom. These varieties are a mixed blessing, however. They look quite impressive from a distance, due to the denseness of the flower head, but this means the spent flowers don't drop off as tidily as the single six-petal kind.

There is a lovely late-blooming plant called 'Heirloom Lace,' which has a peachy glow. As a matter of fact, you can have daylilies right into the fall if you plant the right ones. Then there is 'Pure Light,' white flashed with yellow. If you like reds, try 'Ruby Throat,' which has great clarity (can do with some shade in the afternoon, if you can manage it), and 'Scarlet Tanager,' which is a real burst of red.

Not to be outdone, the wild pink rambling roses along the edge of the property have begun to open. These grow in with wild honeysuckle. Both are determined plants, so it is a standoff between them. They seem to have struck a sensible balance. These particular roses unfortunately have no odor, so the honeysuckle, in addition to looking like a waterfall of flowers, helps to fill the fragrance gap that there would be otherwise.

Wild honeysuckle, which most people have and which you see everwhere, is Hall's Japanese honeysuckle. It is almost a weed and can really take over. Don't let it get started where you don't want it. If you do want to plant honeysuckle, there are two fragrant varieties (and the odor, more than anything else, is what I like about it): 'Dropmore Scarlet,' which is red instead of the more traditional color—hardy in Zones 3–9 (it was developed in Canada)—and 'Serotina Florida.' This is my choice of the two, because it not only is fragrant and has beautiful flowers, which are pink in bud and turn white when they open, but it is controllable and will stay within bounds, being almost as hardy as 'Dropmore.' Zones 5–9.

For a better "wild type" rose, there is one called 'The Fairy.' It is strong and healthy and spreads over walls and grows in great rolling heaps. 'Seafoam' is its white cousin. Both are disease-resistant (important because when it gets going, it would be too much to spray), and grow in Zones 5–10. There is a paler pink that can stand shade and is also hardy, called 'Gruss an Aachen.'

Beginning to flower now are the verbenas. This year I used all the old flowerpots of every size I had, and planted pink verbenas in them—grouping them around the dwarf pines on the decks. To keep this from being too monotonous, I added a few dark purples spotted among the pink. Although this is a favorite flower of mine, I don't plant it every year, planting pinks or cream-colored lantanas on the decks some summers instead. I tried geraniums years back, but didn't like them as well. Same with petunias, which tend to get too knocked around by the wind. Impatiens suffers a similar fate. I'm sure there is a spot around where both of these would be comfortable, but I haven't found it.

A friend gave me a big bunch of calendulas to photograph this week, because only one or two of mine from last year had reseeded. They have been reseeding every spring for the last four years, but I imagine they have finally just run out. Many things will reseed, so be on the lookout for seedlings, even at this late date. Any you find now will just be coming into bloom in August. Calendulas are an exception. They are really fast growers, being in bloom very quickly after you begin to find the first plants—and fertilize them. They also transplant well.

Reminders

☐ Japanese beetles are about to appear and will have to be dealt with. There is divided opinion about this. Some people say that having those unsightly traps swinging in the breeze actually attracts more of these omnivorous pests. If you use traps, at least place them out of sight. They are not like a birdhouse, and ruin the look of the garden if stuck smack in the middle of a rose bed. Unfortunately, beetles love roses. They present a disgusting spectacle when they infest the flowers. I often go out early in the morning and pick off as many as I can by hand. It is usually a losing battle, but they will finally disappear as unexpectedly as they came.

☐ It's time to check your mulch. About now, it has probably gotten scattered around, so should be patched up before the hottest weather comes. Everything but the irises benefits from this.

☐ Fertilize perennials and shrubs for the last time this year. You don't want to encourage new growth much after the middle of this month, because it is time for these plants to start hardening off for the fall and their winter rest. The opposite is true of annuals. They should be fed right up to the end, to stay healthy and blooming. (Remember, however, when I say you shouldn't fertilize perennials after this week that I am talking about Zones 6 and 7, which is roughly where I am situated.)

☐ If you have holes in your flower beds where things have died or been cut back, try planting lettuce seed. It sprouts very quickly this time of the year, but must be watered regularly to get established. Planted now, it will make a nice late-fall crop, and look pretty in the meantime.

Start making a bouquet of this sort by lining the large open container with oasis bricks. I always put in the "feathery" flowers first, in this case the sea lavender (Goniolimon tataricum 'Dumosa'), which is a lovely gray plant that dries well. Zones 4–7. Next comes the yellow yarrow (Achillea millefolium), which also dries well. Zones 3–9. Finally, in go the small, white, daisy-like flowers called feverfew (Chrysanthemum parthenium). Zones 4–8.

These 'Sterling Star' lilies were first stuck into a layer of oasis, which was then covered with black pebbles. They will keep opening on the stem. Cut off old ones as they fade. Zones 3–9.

To make this bouquet, I placed a piece of crumpled chicken wire in the top of the large-mouthed container to support all the flowers' stems. Baby's breath (Gypsophila paniculata), Zones 3–9, went in first. Then the 'Gold Bound' Japanese iris (Iris kaempferi) and Shasta daisies (Chrysanthemum superbum), Zones 5–9 (Zone 4 with protection).

Because the mouth of this container is so wide, I put crumpled chicken wire in it before the white cleomes, white snapdragons (Antirrhinum), and mixed cream and white zinnias. This was a long-lasting bouquet. All are annuals.

The Third Week of July

A single viola

Japanese iris

Two kinds of hydrangeas

The Third Week of July

We cut off the last white foxglove this week and saw the final Japanese iris . . . and speaking of irises, this is the beginning of the time when you should divide and transplant them (and plant new varieties). You can continue until well into August. Actually, irises will survive a move later than that, but they won't make much progress the following year. If you like irises as much as I do, you can have them for six weeks by planting several kinds that will bloom after one another.

Before listing the various ones you might want to try, let me give you a little simple information about planting. What follows technically applies to bearded (or German) irises, but conditions are similar for all varieties.

First be sure the spot you choose to plant in has at least a half day of good strong sun. Allow a space about 16 inches square for each. This may seem to place them far apart, but they multiply rapidly, and it is easy to keep them weed-free this way. Dig some organic material into the soil (but no manure—irises are subject to borers, and rot and manure is too rich for them). I'm told bearded irises don't like acidity. I've never tested my soil, but it seems to be all right. I don't think they can be too fussy. If you know your soil is very acid, you may add bone meal to balance it. Since I feed my irises with this anyway, the problem is automatically taken care of, if it exists. Now make a hole about 2 inches deep and put a mound of earth in the middle. Place the iris rhizome (tuber-like) on it and let the roots spread out in the hole around it. Cover these lightly with soil, leaving the rhizome partly exposed. This is how they like to stay. Shallow planting helps to keep rotting to a minimum and to discourage borers. Irises look best if planted in groups of one color (with an accent or two), but even single plants become groups very quickly.

Plant other varieties the same way, basically. You can mulch all irises except the bearded ones.

To divide and transplant, shake the dirt from the rhizome and roots. Cut out any old or mushy portions. Often a clump will fall into several major parts as you are handling it. Cut the leaves off about 6 inches from the ground, in a fan shape. Some people say it is a good idea to leave irises uprooted in the sun for a day, to get rid of insects.

Siberian irises grow in such dense clumps that you almost have to chop them apart; same with some of the Japanese. Don't be timid about this. As above, inspect them for pests and rot.

If you have never grown irises before, don't go overboard until you have a chance to see how they grow and what color range you like. Pictures in catalogs can be deceiving, and as you get to know a species of plant you often change your mind about its possibilities.

I've already mentioned bearded irises, and these are the first to bloom. Japanese irises are the last, with others falling in between and overlapping. The exception is *Iris cristata,* which is "wild" and blooms in the spring.

SIBERIAN IRIS. This is the hardiest species, but they have a more limited color range than the bearded. Mostly blue purple and whites. They need to have their old foliage cut down annually (either late fall—which avoids the sight of their foliage all winter—or early spring). They like a more acid soil and more moisture than bearded. Really tough—wonderful for naturalizing. Zones 2–8.

JAPANESE IRIS *(Iris kaempferi).* These beauties are sometimes called orchid iris, because their flowers are so exotic. They are also fine cut flowers. Like their Siberian brothers, these like a more acid soil and some moisture in droughts. The color range is white to blue purple, but much more subtle than Siberian. There is now a pink, which I'm told is beautiful, called 'Pink Frost.' Available from White Flower Farm. Zones 5–9.

IRIS PSEUDACORUS. This is the yellow flag iris of swamps and wetlands and is related to Louisiana iris, which, incidentally, is now being grown in a much larger variety of colors than before. Zones 4–9.

IRIS PALLIDA 'VARIEGATA.' This variety has rather "chic" foliage, which can add a dash of zip to a border, and is grown same as bearded iris. Needs sun. Zones 4–9.

IRIS CRISTATA. This is the "wild" one I mentioned earlier. Blooming in the spring with a mass of small light blue flowers. It makes a good ground cover. Zones 3–9.

Two beautiful wildflowers are blooming in combination this week: Queen Anne's lace and blue chicory. Chicory roots can be roasted and ground and are a popular addition to ordinary coffee grinds in Louisiana. The flowers aren't much good in bouquets but are a beautiful shade of blue in the wild. Queen Anne's lace is in the carrot family, with a long root. This can be a pain in the cultivated garden. They are best appreciated in a meadow or along the road. However, they do make good cut flowers. Give them time to revive after they are cut, because they tend to droop for a couple of hours.

Reminders

☐ If you haven't pruned your spring-blooming shrubs yet, you had better get to it. This is good to do in the late afternoon, when it has cooled down. While you have the shears handy, take a look at all the beds and thin them out to keep the air circulation going.

☐ The spring bulb catalogs start arriving about now. I often see people sitting on the beach around here poring over them—which always amuses me for some reason. But it is probably a good idea to take a quick look if you are in the market for bulbs. There are often incentive discounts for early orders. Don't go overboard if you are inexperienced. Bulbs don't plant themselves.

☐ Butterfly bush plants usually start arriving at the nurseries about now, so if you are in the market for this lovely plant, take a look.

☐ And keep watering.

Japanese iris (Iris kaempferi) in the garden with wild daisies, spires of white mullein (Verbascum chaixii 'Album'), Zones 5–9, white foxglove (Digitalis), Zones 3–8, and rosy pink checkerbloom (Sidalcea), Zones 5–9.

This little purple viola (Viola cornuta) has been growing in my garden for four years, reseeding and multiplying each spring. Zones 6–9 (farther north with protection).

The pale blue/white Japanese iris is I. kaempferi 'Ise,' the white with yellow throat is 'Gold Bound,' and the very dark purple blue is 'Nara'—all about 40 inches tall. Zones 4–9. To the right are the Siberian iris (I. sibirica). These include 'Caesar's Brother' (dark blue), 'Flight of Butterflies,' and 'Skywings,' which is very pale blue with white. Zones 3–9.

To keep these hydrangeas (H. macrophylla) under control, I tied them together before putting them in the container. Hydrangeas are shrubs, hardy in Zones 7–9, and grow to a height of 4 feet or more, but can be pruned to a convenient size. There are two kinds here. The flatter one with a small central mass of flowers is 'Blue Lace' and the other is the standard blue mophead form, of which Wayside's 'All Summer Beauty' is a good kind. To keep these plants blue, make a solution of ¼ ounce of aluminum sulfate and ¼ ounce of iron sulfate to 1 gallon of water, and soak the soil several times at weekly intervals in the spring and again in the fall.

Gloriosa-daisies and calendulas

Tricolor chrysanthemums

Vases containing coreopsis, cockscomb, everlasting, and lilies

Mixed zinnias

Mixed snapdragons

Annual dwarf phlox

Bachelor's-buttons

Calla lilies in mixed bouquets

The Last Week of July

The Last Week of July

Somehow years ago when I was moving plants from a friend's garden to mine, unbeknownst to me I got a few "wild" orange tiger lilies in the bargain. From that accidental planting, I have several very large patches of them—one of which came from what was left over in a bed from which I thought I'd dug them all. After the second year they were once again so dense there I couldn't even tell I had moved any. They must certainly be the hardiest lily to grow in this vicinity. I'm told that Indians used to eat its white bulbs, which become quite large. Unlike others of its strain, they are so sturdy they are almost rabbit-proof. Which is going some. And they make wonderful cut flowers. But this is a bit of a cautionary tale. I'm lucky my lilies, which are just opening now, are growing more or less where I want them. Getting rid of an established clump would be quite a task.

Also still in bloom are the remarkable little purple vincas, which first started in April. By the middle of next month, their long arms of foliage (and flowers) will start to get rather stringy. In the meantime, a mound of fresh leaves will have formed at each clump's middle. It is when this mound appears that I begin cutting off the older growth. A few weeks after that they will be starting all over again, and will continue until frost. The small stock plants and dark salvias that I added to the vinca bed are still carrying on.

I have baby's breath in bloom in the cutting garden. I like it for bouquets, but not so much in a perennial bed, where it looks too floppy to suit me. However, they are easy and worth growing. 'Bristol Fairy' is the tallest (about 4 feet) and is not only good in the house, but quite good for drying. There is also a pink version, called 'Pink Fairy,' that is shorter (about a foot and a half). If you see *Gypsophila paniculata* 'Perfecta' plants around, try one. This has double white flowers and is a strong grower. Should you not be putting it in a cutting garden, think carefully about where it is to go, because it takes plenty of space and almost always must be staked. It's important to give baby's breath strong support at its base and let it billow out at the top. Because it has such a long taproot, it is almost impossible to move with success. But it is a lot

tougher than its dainty flowers make it look. Zones 3–9.

Another plant that is just now showing buds and that I especially like is false dragonhead. It could almost be called a semiweed, it is so undemanding and simple to get started. Unlike others in this category, which are hardy and spread quickly, it is no problem to keep under control. It can be bought in both white and a lavender pink. In bloom it makes a thicket of lovely spires of color. Zones 3–9.

Reminders

☐ Attend garden center sales. There are usually two sales a year, one about now and another later in the season—say, mid-October. If you have had your eye on certain shrubs or trees and a sale is in progress it's not a bad idea to talk over your requirements with the owner. Sometimes they are anxious to "clear the yard" for the incoming fall plants (mostly evergreens) and will give you a better price, especially if you want several things. This way, you can get your plants and they can get their space. If it's a large garden center, they may plant your purchases for you and guarantee them for the first year—the trees anyway. Should your plant(s) have been sitting around all season and need nursing, it's not likely you'll get the guarantee. You'll then have to be responsible for getting them established, and hope for the best.

Some superior trees to look for are: paper or canoe birch, all the beeches, Japanese dogwood, the katsura tree, goldenrain tree, various magnolias, sourwood tree, Japanese snowbell, Japanese pagoda tree, and Japanese stewartia. Most of these trees are rare, and all are beautiful. If suitable to your climate, they can be a joy—and a lifetime investment.

☐ Water, water, water. At least three times a week—more if possible. And a good soaking each time. There are timers on the market that require no electricity and can turn your hoses on and off for you. Sometimes nursery personnel will set up this system for you. Ask. And don't think you can get by with trying to collect on your guarantee if you have let a plant die through your own neglect. Experienced nurserymen know the difference between neglect and disease.

☐ If you aren't dividing your irises this year, be sure to keep them properly weeded. This is best done after a rain, when the ground isn't so hard and you can usually yank up the offending root with ease. If it doesn't rain, weed after watering—but not when the leaves are still wet through. They say this spreads disease.

Watch out for mildew and mold, which can get going really fast in hot damp weather. When they strike, cut off the worst parts and spray with Benlate or dust with sulfur. This must not be done until the sun is going down, as the combination of a strong medicine and hot sun can really burn a plant. While the good air circulation I keep talking about should do the trick, some seasons are just bad and you get mildew no matter what. If you know that a particular plant is subject to mildew or mold, water the soil around it, keeping as much as possible off the leaves. The early morning of a sunny day is best.

☐ Take cuttings for propagation. It is an extremely easy process. Forsythia, lilac, weigela, and pyracantha are all good candidates. They are hardy enough for you to be almost assured of success. Here's how:

Prepare a shady area in your garden by digging out a spot and filling it with a mixture of half peat moss and half perlite. It should be well drained and close to a water source if you can swing it. You would prepare pots with the same mixture if you would rather use them.

When all is ready, take a cutting about 6 to 8 inches in length. These should be cut just below the spot where the leaf joins the stem (a node). After pulling off the leaves from the lower half, dip the cut end into rooting hormone, which will encourage the growth of roots. If there are any flowers or flower buds, pinch them off. Plant cuttings about 1 or 2 inches deep, and keep them watered. The soil must remain moist.

Some people cover cuttings with clear plastic bags, into which they have punched a few holes, to retain moisture. Make certain the plastic does not come in contact with the cuttings, however.

In four to six weeks you will be able to transplant the newly rooted plants to their permanent spot. Keep them watered and lightly shaded. Put a stake or marker by them, because it is awfully easy to forget where—or that—you have planted the small cuttings. In the spring, fertilize them and stand back.

Gloriosa-daisies (Rudbeckia hirta), with dark centers and multipetaled calendulas (Calendula officinalis) are both annuals and easy to grow. They want good light but are not particular about growing conditions. Gloriosas can be treated as perennials in some situations, but for assured bloom, plant some early every spring. They reach a height of 3 feet. Calendulas reach a height of 18 inches and will reseed themselves if allowed to. They will also continue to bloom most of the summer if you keep dead flowers cut.

The small vase on the left holds a variety of tickseed (Coreopsis) with a brown eye. Height 2 feet. Zones 3–10. In the jug next to it is annual cockscomb (Celosia cristata 'Golden Triumph'). Height 18 inches to 2 feet. The yellow lilies at the back are 'Connecticut King.' And at top left is an annual perfect for drying, called everlasting (Limonium). Height 2½ feet.

Zinnias are one of my favorite cut flowers. These natives of Mexico are extremely easy to grow and germinate rapidly (three to four days). They need to be fertilized regularly, and deadheaded as well. Picking flowers for bouquets is the best way to keep them happy! Pictured here is a selection of beauties from Burpee's giant flowering mixture.

Annual chrysanthemum (Chrysanthemum carinatum) prefers coolish summers and a heavy soil. Burpee's 'Rainbow Mix,' seen here, is a good one. Height 2 feet.

Snapdragons (Antirrhinum) are annuals that grow best in cooler weather and will give two strong shows of color if cut regularly, fed, and watered. Taller varieties may need staking. Here you see an old-fashioned variety mixed with the newer "open face" kind (in pink) called 'Wedding Bells' in the center of the bouquet.

I had to put a little oasis in these vases to make the flowers stay where I wanted them. Aside from the pink and yellow calla lilies (Zantedeschia), there are pink eustomas (E. grandiflorum), pink, multipetaled ranunculus, and pink larkspur (Delphinium). The callas and ranunculus must be planted each year from bulbs. Eustoma and larkspur are annuals.

I first tied this bunch of mixed dwarf phlox (Phlox drummondii 'Dwarf Beauty') (7 inches) and then cut the stems so that the bouquet could sit comfortably in the wide-mouthed compote dish. This strain is annual.

The mixed bachelor's-buttons (Centaurea cyanus) are also known as cornflower. The ones here are the tall variety (2½ feet), but there is a shorter variety too.

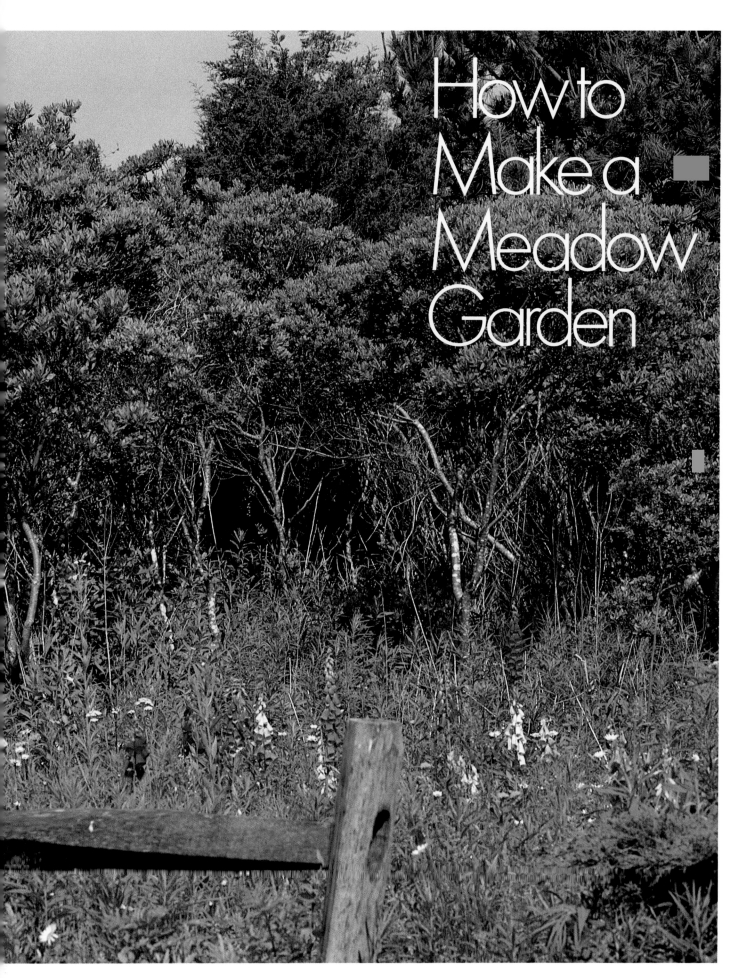

How to Make a Meadow Garden

How to Make a Meadow Garden

The meadow garden is what I refer to as my weed garden. In the past, a number of people have asked me for advice about the best way of dealing with a meadow. I suppose this is because my house is situated right in the middle of one and over the years I have seemed to be fooling with it all the time.

First, let me make a distinction. If you recall, I said in the introduction that I made a decision when I first built my house to put only a small part of the land into lawn and to leave the balance in a wild state—or semiwild. My technique for dealing with it then was more or less passive. That is, I let the birds and wind bring in seeds, then worked with the results.

This meant that I had to pull out what I didn't like or had to try to stop the spread of things that were getting too rampant. For instance, wild brambles started in a spot where they weren't welcome and they had to be dealt with. This was something that I couldn't let go on for too long, because once undesirables gain too strong a hold, they can become almost impossible to eradicate. This is especially true with bittersweet vine. Even desirable plants like *Rosa rugosa* can be pesky. What this method requires is a sharp eye and a flexible attitude. One of the great pleasures of all this is that you never quite know from year to year what you will have to handle. Or what wonders will occur. The only thing I regularly do is to have it all mowed down in the late fall (rugosa, too). I have, at times, left the cut plants lying there all winter, then raked them off in the spring before the daffodils put their buds up. Mowing means you will always have a few weeks very early in the year when things look barren—before the meadow sprouts. It is really better to rake right after mowing, but if you don't get to it all is not lost. Once the meadow has grown in, I let this go for a few months and then have it mowed in selected areas, which change

Overleaf: *Foxgloves naturalized in an area of my garden*

slightly from year to year, depending on what has popped up. The only thing I have consciously tried to naturalize overall are daisies and, to a lesser degree, black-eyed Susans. In some places I have put in daffodils, and under the pines I put wild geraniums, poppies, irises, miniature daffodils, and wood hyacinths. In an even smaller space, I've gotten foxgloves going.

But there is another way. That is to start the project by having the area rototilled after cutting and raking it first. This is absolutely necessary to do if you plan to broadcast most wildflower seeds—or those hybrids that will naturalize and reseed themselves. I see big bags of regional wildflower seeds advertised in catalogs all the time. To judge from reading the copy, all you have to do is run across the hills like Maria in *The Sound of Music* gaily broadcasting seeds about. This is nonsense. You get almost no results this way.

Seeding can be done in the fall and spring. You may use a mixture you make yourself or experiment with single-flower areas. In addition to wildflowers like yarrow, gaillardia, lupine, and coreopsis, it is possible to grow spring-flowering bulbs. These should not be planted until you have got your meadow going, because after planting you will not be able to rototill again. Bulbs should be ordered as early as possible, and are best when they are mixtures of specific ones you make yourself, rather than those prepackaged general mixtures. Also, remember to select those bulbs that will bloom at intervals. They should be planted in September in order for them to establish good root systems before cold weather sets in. But if you wait until the season almost ends, there are bargains to be had at garden centers. Bulbs planted later usually bloom late the first year (and sometimes not as profusely), but fall into a normal pattern after they are established. The main thing is to get the daffodils planted in clumps and not scattered around the landscape in polka dots. Instructions for planting bulbs can be found in the September section of this book.

The one rule for this aggressive approach (aside from rototilling) is mowing. Unmowed meadows are not gardens, but slums of tall-growing weeds and small weed trees and shrubs. In addition to mowing, there is raking. Tall grass left lying smothers the growth of wanted, planted plants during their growing season. The average meadow garden, in a climate with average rainfall, needs to be mowed three times each year: once in late June after the bulb foliage has died back, once in late summer (early September), and finally in late fall (November). This last mowing is not only so you can start with a clean slate in spring, but so the bulbs can easily be seen as they come in. The drier the climate and poorer the soil, the less necessary mowing is. But as a rule of thumb, three times is about right.

Some plants that work in meadows are columbine, butterfly weed, various asters, echinacea, helianthus (which are in the sunflower family), bee balm or monarda, rudbeckia or black-eyed Susan, and foxglove. If you grow some of the later-flowering plants, you must vary your mowing schedule for their time of bloom. Or perhaps contain them in an area that is separate. The whole process just requires a little thought and common sense. All the things mentioned are hardy and will reseed themselves—and of course there are others. There are also plants such as bachelor's button that will thrive for a time and eventually run out (instead of really naturalizing). Planting these will require you to rototill every few years.

After planting, pray for rain. This is the variable you can't do anything about. A damp spring is a must.

A final word: do not fertilize. Poor soil is best.

Wild mustard and garlic mustard

Butter-and-eggs and wild indigo

Cinquefoil and wild honeysuckle

Knapweed, Queen Anne's lace, blue vervain, and dill blossoms

100 / COUNTRY FLOWERS

Yellow buttercup, cypress spurge, and wild grass

Wild phlox and clover

Swamp honeysuckle and wild beach pea

Lupine, columbine, red clover, and beach pea

Roadside
Bouquets

Roadside Bouquets

I have always made what I call roadside bouquets, but until I decided to devote a little special section to them, I had never actually realized how much there is out there. This year was certainly a revelation on that score. I can now spot a flash of pink or yellow from the corner of my eye while going fifty miles an hour and talking a blue streak. Probably one of the things that keeps many of us from noticing this wonderful variety is that we ignore those little flashes of color—usually being too occupied to slow down or to back up for a closer inspection. I discovered plants this season that I had never been aware of during the past twenty years of driving the same back roads on Long Island.

There isn't too much advice I can give on how to find things to include in these appealing little bouquets except "be prepared." Have a bucket of water and a pair of clippers at the ready at all times. Both are important. You don't want to risk uprooting wild plants, so clippers are a must—and water is an equal necessity. Many wildflowers are fragile, and if the day is hot they would not make it back to the house before being completely wilted, were they not standing with their feet in cool water. Even under the best of circumstances, many will droop somewhat; but, given time, they will usually come around.

Fall is a very good time to gather stems and seed pods to make fall bouquets. The trick here is to have enough of the same thing to make a statement. I remember one year I never got around to cutting out all the old dead flower stems in a daylily border. One weekend a friend asked if he could cut them. Naturally, I was delighted—and doubly pleased when I saw the spectacular bouquet they turned into in the city. The stems and pods don't look like much individually, but in a big group they take on a whole new dimension.

I notice, too, that in the fall these wild bouquets seem to get larger and larger. I suppose with things like goldenrod and wild asters to use, along with all the tall grasses around, this is inevitable.

The only drawback about wildflowers is that you never know how long they will hold in the house— unless, of course, you have gathered ones you are familiar with. So don't be discouraged if a bouquet that looks beautiful when you go to bed gives up the ghost during the night. Press on.

I understand that you find yellow wild mustard, also called common winter cress, growing over a large part of the country where damp springs are typical. I've been told you can use its leaves in salad, although they are said to be quite bitter. I didn't have much luck trying to identify the white weed. It could be white baneberry.

The five petal yellow flower is cinquefoil (Potentilla) which grows in the dryer areas from Virginia to New England and west to Tennessee. It usually indicates poor soil. Wild Japanese honeysuckle (Lonicera japonica) is a climbing vine everyone knows. It escaped from cultivation years ago and can be found almost all over the United States. It is reported to be able to grow up to 30 feet in a single season.

The small flowers which look like miniature snapdragons are butter-and-eggs (Linaria vulgaris). It grows most places and has a very long blooming period, usually beginning around June and continuing into August. It does well in dry areas and is easy to get started if you gather the dry seeds. The large yellow trumpet flower is wild indigo (Baptisia tinctoria) which likes about the same conditions as butter-and-eggs and can be found from New England to Florida and west to Louisiana and then up to Minnesota.

The pinkish thistle-like flower is spotted knapweed (Centurea maculosa), and I understand it grows all over the east. Queen Anne's lace, also called wild carrot, grows over an even wider area—almost from coast to coast. Same with blue vervain. The yellowish dill blossoms belong to the same family as Queen Anne's lace.

The lovely small yellow buttercup (Ranunculus acris) is found almost any place there is moist soil—especially after a damp spring. Juice from its stems is acrid, hence 'acris,' discouraging browsing animals and favoring its spread. Cypress spurge (Euphorbia cyparissias) is in the same family as the Christmas poinsettia. Its sap can cause dermatitis in some people, so wash your hands thoroughly after handling it. The dark brownish-red tufts are just wild grass that I liked the color of.

Swamp honeysuckle (Rhododendron viscosum) is sometimes called clammy azalea because of its sticky petals. The species name means "sticky" in Latin. It prefers damp, even swampy, conditions and can be found from Maine to Georgia and as far west as Texas. In the small container are multi-colored beach peas.

Wild phlox or sweet rocket (Hesperis matronalis) grows to 2 or 3 feet and spreads rapidly. Around here it blooms for almost the whole month of June in large clumps beside the road. Red clover (Trifolium pratense) is a member of the pea family and blooms off and on from May to September. You see it everywhere because it is used to improve soil in rotation—its roots store nitrogen, which refreshes the fields.

The blue flower is wild lupine (there is a bit more about it in "A Walk in the Woods," page 49) and the yellow and orange is wild columbine. Both of these are worth growing in their hybridized form. They like shade in the hottest part of the day and benefit from plenty of water. Red clover, you probably recognize, and the beach pea looks like its glamorous cousin, the sweet pea.

AUGUST

Overleaf: *August . . . and the living is easy*

AUGUST

I think everyone must have a memory or two from the distant past that is so indelibly planted that a key word or situation always elicits the same automatic reaction. When you say "August" to me in the general context of the weather or the summer season, I invariably think of dusty sidewalks and of hearing someone practicing the piano. There is nothing arcane about this response. As a matter of fact, the specific memory is so pleasant, I often stop when it comes to mind and relive it.

August in Louisiana is tremendously hot, and the air is often very still. And in the pre-air-conditioning days from which this memory flows, no one was ever stirring outside in the afternoon but kids before they had to take their naps and people (in the shadow of their umbrellas) on unavoidable errands. Everyone else dozed in the relentless heat, moving as little as possible. But I was allowed to go crawfishing then, which was one of my all-time favorite pastimes. The best place was in the bayou in back of the cemetery. Of course, this was the same bayou that ran through our property a half mile away, but it was better and more mysterious out by the quiet resting place of my small town's founding fathers and their progeny. My route for getting there took me across the empty lot behind the Methodist church, past my best friend Sonny Carter's house—where I could then safely take off my sandals (out of view of my mother, who had forbidden me to go barefoot—"common," she said) and drag my feet in the cut grass that had been thrown up on the sidewalk by the mower, where it had parched. The little ritual made a dry, dusty sound as grass scraped along the cement. And just as I passed the house next to the rectory where the living-room window always was thrown open (or so it seemed), I could hear scales being practiced or some piece being laboriously played on the piano. For whatever reason, the memory of this seems unbearably sweet. Although I can see it as clearly as if it had taken place yesterday (it was actually almost exactly a half century ago), I sometimes wonder if it ever really happened. I still love to hear the piano being practiced somewhere off in the distance. And it was only a few years later that I had that first wonderfully confusing flushed feeling at the sight of a girl named Alice who played the piano in a recital held in that same Methodist church.

The reality of August for me today is, of course, totally different—and especially from a gardening standpoint. It is more likely than not just a continuation of July. Lots of weeding and watering and grooming. Many of the flowers are, or are about to be, completing their cycles. Butterfly bush is out, but by month's end, aside from chrysanthemums and Montauk daisies, there will not be much left in my beds to come into bloom that has not already shown its color.

I can expect to see more roses off and on until frost, and sometimes a few of the perennials will do a brief reprise. But beginning around the third week, the action starts to shift toward the meadow, where it all began, with a splendid display of wild asters and goldenrod, of which I counted more than seven varieties one year. Whenever I think of them, I think of my poor father and his hay fever. What a time the approach of fall was for him. Our house was always filled with yellow goldenrod mixed with lavender blue asters (wild), courtesy of my mother, who loved big bouquets. And since he loved her and thought almost everything she did was OK, he just sneezed and bore up through her decorating enthusiasms.

I know a lot of people talk about collecting seeds to plant the next year. For wild things like daisies and black-eyed Susans, this is fine. But for hybrids of different colors it is pointless; because of the cross-pollination, you are unlikely to get the flower in the color you want. The only seeds I collect are for Iceland poppies. I don't care how the colors get mixed up, you need so many seeds (and they are so fine) to broadcast them over a sizable area that it is worth the uncertainty. And poppies don't like to be transplanted. Even the very young seedling has an extremely long root, which is almost impossible not to disturb when you dig it. Incidentally, remember this is one plant that you almost have to plant in the fall if you want to get good results.

So August it is—the last full month of summer.

Mixed larkspur

Blue lace flower, salvia, and velvet flower

A basketload of August's finest

A basket of cosmos

Mixed cleome

Sunrise on a misty morning

The First Week of August

The First Week of August

All the old yellow daylilies on the bank have just about finished, leaving behind a sea of stems. These will be cut to neaten up the bed, and also to keep plants from squandering their strength supporting these now useless stalks. And in some cases to make seedpods. You should always do the same with your own daylily bed. While you are at it, this is also the time to give the bed a good general weeding.

The later dark red daylilies along the drive are still going strong. Growing large quantities of varieties with different blooming times in these separate areas makes it possible to have an impressive display of lilies for almost six weeks—beginning with yellow and orange and ending with the dark reds. Some gardeners mix late- and early-blooming ones in the same border, but I don't particularly like doing this. I want a dense swath of color. And you can have this only with one or two kinds together, which are on similar blooming schedules—leaving no holes. I enjoy the changing emphasis this places on the garden, too.

August began in a rather soggy way and continued to be partly hazy with occasional light showers (I sound like a weather forecaster)—which you could see in the distance and could smell coming as the wind freshened. While this might not be the sort of weather vacationers dream of, it is perfect for rearranging plants. If you don't mind getting wet and sometimes slightly muddy, all this dampness guarantees a good survival rate for transplants. You remember I said earlier that you should take a critical look at your borders as they come into bloom and make notes on which plants are crowding or screening others. This is a continuing process. You never know when a particular perennial will take off and grow like crazy while another, which is supposedly hardy and tall, will decide not to cooperate. There will be more on this next month.

In the spring I planted pink calla lilies in the cutting garden to keep them out of harm's way (rabbits!) until they were mature. Now that they are in bloom, I have moved them out into the bed for a touch of extra color. The best way to transplant fully developed annuals is one or two at a time. Dig the holes you are going to put them in before you dig the plant. Then you can just plop it right in. Pack dirt around the base with your foot, pushing down hard. Transplanted this way, plants will be out of the ground less than ten minutes. And if you do it in between showers, they will probably just think they were having a nightmare and continue to grow and bloom without even wilting.

This is also the sort of weather to pull long-established weeds that might be plaguing your semiwild beds. Most will come right out, root and all, with a good tug. When the ground is dry and hard, you generally just break off the top, leaving their root to sprout again. If this task doesn't appeal to you, forget it and go to the movies with the kids.

I planted a number of different kinds of sunflowers in the cutting garden early in the spring. This is really the only place they work for me, because of their height. I tried them close to a post at the end of the deck one year and they looked all right for a time, but the plant itself got ugly as it started losing its lower leaves. Probably an ideal spot would be in back of a fence about 4 feet tall. That way you would just see the tops. Anyway, I am particularly partial to them as cut flowers, and there are a surprising number of varieties. They are listed under their botanical name *(Helianthus)* in some seed catalogs if you have trouble finding them. My favorites are 'Autumn Beauty,' 6-foot plants that make lots of gold, bronze, bright yellow, and mahogany-colored flowers about 6 inches in diameter. And I always grow the shorter variety called 'Italian White.' These aren't actually white, but a very light yellow flower with dark centers. Then there is 'Piccolo,' which is only about 4 feet high, but throws out lots of yellow flowers with dark centers. The only problem you face with these old favorites is wind. Once they have been knocked over, you can seldom right them. However, if you have the space to leave them where they have fallen, usually they will continue to send up flowers to face the sun. Another variety worth trying is the 'Sunburst' mix—it is similar to 'Autumn Beauty,' but not as tall.

In spite of the overcast weather, the sun-lovers are at their peak—mostly in shades of yellow. In addition to black-eyed Susans and the aforementioned *Helianthus*, there are *Helenium* and *Heliopsis* (all named for the Greek sun god Helios) all blazing away. These are somewhat spurned by sophisticated gardeners, but surely are easy in the back of a border (except for the taller varieties of *Helianthus*), and look even better when their color is tempered with some of the easy whites like baby's breath (planted in such a way that its shape isn't too important) and phlox. Remember that all these plants are susceptible to mildew, so give them room to breathe. Another plant that is good for a no-work area is meadow rue. All these plants are OK in Zones 3–9—a good wide range.

Even with cloud cover, the temperature has been soaring. The heat made me think about the plants that have a Mediterranean quality to them. These often work well close to a pool, where there is a lot of reflected heat. If this appeals to you, have a look at the yuccas, which would be sending up their spikes of flowers right now. There is a variegated one called 'Bright Edge' that you might like. Then there is something called red-hot poker, which looks just like what you would imagine. I understand it has been hybridized in the last few years for extra hardiness, and they continue to bloom well into September. A cactus that you see around is prickly pear, which makes red fruits this month. And for a bit of softness amid all these spikes you should plant sedums to creep around and blur the edges. All these need to be grown in well-drained soil and strong light. If you have a fence and want a vine on it, you might plant trumpet vine. It is extremely hardy and is usually seen in yellow or bright orange, but it can be gotten in cream as well. Though probably the yellow would work nicely with the other colors.

This is a low point for roses, off of which I have cut the dying flowers—encouraging them to put out new growth. They are full of buds and will be giving me a new crop soon, to continue off and on until frost.

The little patch of volunteer snapdragons that came up by the deck, which I mentioned finding a while back are now beginning to open. They are still very short but probably sense they had better get on with it. The color is a kind of rusty orange with a touch of pink at the mouth, a color combination that has nothing to do with the ones that seeded them last year.

Larkspur (Delphinium) *is an annual that blooms in shades of pink, blue, and white and reaches a height of 3 to 4 feet. It thrives in cool spring weather, and runs out of steam when it gets really hot. Give it plenty of water and shade from afternoon sun for best results.*

This bouquet includes snapdragons (Antirrhinum majus 'White Rocket'), *scabiosas, and shaggy as well as daisy-type asters. All are hardy and all are annuals.*

Spider plant (Cleome). *These interesting flowers must be picked in the morning. If picked later and brought inside they will wilt, but will perk up after three or four hours. If you grow them, leave plenty of room between plants. In a border they may need staking.*

The heavily veined, petunia-like flowers are called velvet flower (Salpiglossis). *Colors are very rich, and it grows to a height of 2½ feet. Blue lace flower* (Trachymene coerulea) *looks like a small-scale, blue Queen Anne's lace (also 2½ feet). The spires are blue salvia* (Salvia farinacea), *which has a good strong color, lasts well, and grows to 1½ feet.*

Cosmos 'Sensation' is a very satisfactory annual that grows to approximately 4 feet. They don't require much in the way of special attention except for deadheading. This can be accomplished, at least partially, by cutting them for bouquets. However, if you want really large bouquets, better put them in the cutting garden as well as the beds. Blooms are mainly in shades of rose and pink, with an occasional white.

Marigolds and zinnias

China asters

Tiger and 'Ivory Princess' lilies

Bright orange marigolds

The Second Week of August

The Second Week of August

Driving to the village, I pass several manicured yards that rely heavily on impatiens plants for color to play against their permanent backdrop of evergreens. These plantings are a wonderful mix of colors and seem to thrive in the circumstances under which they are grown, being almost constantly in full flower. A sight marvelous to see the first few weeks. But after passing the same tableau a number of times I realized that by settling for such a limited—though obviously easy—choice, their owners were missing one of the subtle joys of the garden: change. If you notice, I have mentioned on more than one occasion how the focus is constantly switching to a bed just coming into bloom from one that is finishing, and being readied for the next round of color. For me this keeps the garden fresh, and my enthusiasm for it alive. As is almost always the case, you will cease to see a thing that never changes. Don't ever allow your garden to become static. It can grow and mature, but should be forever evolving. You must never be "finished."

Speaking of change, a large patch of black-eyed Susans decided to come up and bloom in the daylily bed on the bank. They started to open about when the last few lilies were finishing. Unfortunately, rabbits love the tenderer members of this yellow daisy-like genus, called rudbeckia. But since rabbits stay out of my dense daylily beds (they run through them, but don't stop to dine), the lilies form a protected environment for the black-eyed Susans—which come into bloom at such a convenient time (right after the lilies). Following their signal, I've moved some of their hybridized relatives into a few open spaces in the bank, which I had originally intended to fill in with more daylilies. This is a perfect example of how plants will let you know where they want to grow. I always heed such advice, and try to expand on it. Keep it in mind.

August usually provides us with periods of scorching weather, and this year the weather is right on target. When I complain about how hot it is to a fellow garden enthusiast, she tells me to think of something cool, like shades of blue. Well, that is as good advice as anything, I suppose, so maybe now is the time to think of bluish flowers and plants. I say bluish because there is very little real blue in flowers. It almost all has a touch of red in it, which sends it off in the direction of lavender. Anyway, in the dappled light you can grow hostas, some of which have a bluish cast to their foliage. Especially *H. sieboldiana* 'Elegans.' This is hardy in Zones 3–10—a very wide range indeed. Or there is the white-flowered *H. plantaginea* 'Grandiflora,' which has a more vibrant green leaf. Both have elegant and fragrant flowers, and are worth tracking down. Balloonflower will grow in the cool shade and give a bit of muscle to the border. Hardy in Zones 3–9, it is best in blue, but also comes in pale pink as well as white. Buy it in the single form which is less likely to topple over. The double flowers tend to be awkward.

For sun, try globe thistle, 'Taplow Blue.' This tame beauty grows well in poor soil and almost everywhere. Its leaves are also a plus. Salvias are worth considering too. Fine August bloomers, they are especially nice in the small-scale blue variety.

My phlox are now going strong, covered with large pink heads of flowers. They are susceptible to mildew, and with all the rain this year, I thought I would certainly have a battle on my hands. But they got through unscathed. It is crucial to deadhead these plants after they finish blooming. Otherwise, you'll have magenta flowers next year and wonder why.

About now houseplants often begin getting leggy and overgrown. These are best pruned of such unwanted or weak shoots. If a plant looks droopy, unpot it to see if there are any bugs nestling in the roots. Get rid of the pests and any diseased or damaged roots, repot it, and reward with a good feeding. Also rotate pots (in case you have forgotten) so that your plants will be good-looking from all sides.

Here we go again: continue to water. Especially roses, which must not ever really become bone dry. They are entering a new blooming cycle, so are especially thirsty. Keep an eye out now for black spot. Take care of it immediately if you come across it. It spreads rapidly.

Every season about now, the cutting garden gets pretty bedraggled. So you should start thinking about clearing out those annuals that are finishing, such as larkspur, overgrown cleome, and annual pinks. Either rototill or pitchfork the soil over to get any lingering pests exposed to the cleansing rays of the sun and then let it settle a bit. Later next month this area will be ready for you to plant something like bulbs.

You may start transplanting wild ferns and other wildflowers now. Just be sure that if you move these from the open woods or a natural habitat you are not digging an endangered or protected species. Always get permission from the property owner, and try not to disturb the location any more than you must. It is also important for you to carefully observe the conditions under which the plants grow naturally. Although it is not completely necessary to duplicate such surroundings to have success—some plants are more adaptable than others—the closer you get the better. Give your spot a good covering of straw to help keep down competition from weeds until plants get established. And in the case of ferns that are planted under trees, straw mulch helps to set off their color. Water generously until fall, but do not fertilize.

This is also a good time to sow seeds of perennial plants that you may want for next year. Two-inch jiffy pots are a good choice. Put them in a plastic tray for stability and use sterilized soil, not soil from the garden. Among the easiest seeds you might want to try are sweet rocket, mallow, loosestrife, speedwell, and gloriosa daisy and its relatives. Keep your seedlings in filtered light according to directions on the package, and above all don't allow them to dry out. As they get larger you may want to put them directly into the ground, where your coldframe can fit over them for protection (from winter's worst) later—or in some cases you can put them directly in the place where they are to grow. This will depend on your climate.

A helpful book for learning all about how to grow plants from seed is by Ann Reilly, called *Park's Success with Seeds,* available through the Park Seed people, P.O. Box 31, Greenwood, SC 29647. Worth the small investment.

The creamy zinnias are called 'Carved Ivory.' Here they are joined by ordinary white zinnias and lovely pale yellow marigolds (Tagetes).

The colors of these China asters (Callistephus chinensis) are marvelous. Start the seeds of this hardy annual inside, but don't plant it in the same spot every year, to avoid wilt.

Lilies need good drainage to really grow well, but are amazingly easy. The shorter hybrids like 'Ivory Princess,' shown here, never need staking. Bright orange naturalized tiger lilies (Lilium lancifolium splendens) are very tall, but so sturdy that they don't need staking either. Most others this height, 3 to 4 feet, will need some support.

These are Burpee Climax hybrid marigolds (Tagetes erecta 'Toreador'). They are annuals and almost too bright for some flower gardens, but are fine cut flowers. Marigolds were discovered growing wild in Mexico by Cortez, who took them back to Spain.

The Third Week of August

Globe thistle and sea holly

The Third Week of August

The traditional August heat wave has finally released its stifling hold. Although the garden has been watered religiously, the sustained extreme weather takes its toll. The situation is not helped by the fact that these August spells usually coincide with the end of many plants' peak growing and blooming cycle—an end that is probably hastened by it all. So circumstances make it more important than ever to get out into the garden and give the beds a good manicuring. I edge them and remove any dead or dying plants and prune those that need it—annuals as well as perennials. After that, I give the beds a light sprinkling of new mulch. This really improves the look of the garden.

The wild areas in front and back of the house are beginning to take on a slight yellowish cast as the goldenrod starts to get ready to bloom. In another week, it should be spectacular. Snapdragons are about up to their last buds and will probably be all finished and ready to be pulled out in another ten days.

Most of the daylilies have faded, and the orange tiger lilies have also opened their last buds. Now is when I have to resist the temptation to let down. I don't set any unrealistic goals for myself, but I make sure to do a few things each day to keep the garden reasonably in shape. There is still lots to enjoy.

If you have any intention of collecting wild daisy seeds to broadcast about, you had better do it soon, before the seed heads dry out too much and shatter. I mentioned earlier that leaving the whole heads intact instead of removing seeds from the center has been more successful for me. I think this is because there is more chance for several of them to germinate and not wash away than when individual seeds are cast about. Safety in numbers. The same is true of black-eyed Susans. However, these are still in bloom, and should be allowed to mature on the stem for another month. They should be ready about this time in September. I'll remind you then.

My *Anemone japonicas,* which I planted for the first time last year, are just beginning to open. And what satisfying plants they are. They make neat little heads of leaves until about the start of this month, when they send up downy gray flower stalks. The variety I have is light pink and is single, although there are other colors and some with more petals. These and the false dragonhead, which I am so fond of, are about the last of my perennials to bloom. There are a few others, of course, and many of the earlier-blooming ones will put out a bit of second bloom to send you off into the fall.

When my old white tree hydrangea started to bloom, I thought about how welcome fall-blooming shrubs can be. There are many fine ones that can lend a bit of blossom to the garden now. Especially good are some of the airier types, such as glossy abelias, chaste tree, butterfly bush, and a little-known clematis in bush form. All are easy to grow and can be bought from knowledgeably run garden centers or the more sophisticated catalogs.

GLOSSY ABELIA (*Abelia grandiflora*). Has a shiny slightly bronze leaf year round except in the more northern parts of its range, where it can die back a bit and will need some late spring (May) clipping to remove winter's dead wood. It requires water during very dry summers. Starting about mid-August, it throws out quantities of tiny pale pink trumpets, and when they go, they leave behind little sepals of equal beauty. Give it mulch in winter, and don't plant it where the wind can do it damage. Incidentally, there is now a dwarf variety on the market, which you can use in tight spots. This grows to about 3 feet instead of the usual 5 feet. Zones 5–8.

CHASTE TREE (*Vitex agnus-castus*). Has lavender blue flowers this time of the year, resembling lilacs. It also has a pretty silvery leaf, which is slightly aromatic. Since it blooms on new growth, should it die back because of a hard winter, just cut it off and it will start all over. A friend tells me she leaves hers alone until mid-May to make sure it isn't going to come out before pruning. Zones 6–9. Height 10 feet.

BUTTERFLY BUSH *(Buddleia davidii)*. I'm particularly fond of these shrubs, especially the darker red purple ones. There are also lighter shades of blue and lavender and a white. They are very tough and, like the chaste tree, don't break their winter dormancy until late spring. But they grow fast. Zones 5–9. Can grow as high as 10 feet.

HERBACCOUS CLEMATIS *(Clematis heracleifolia* 'Davidiana' and *C. heracleifolia* 'Wyevale'). They are not so well known or grown often around here, but are worth searching out for their fragrance and clear blue color. Since they have a low-growing shape, they can go where taller plants wouldn't work. They do well in both sun and shade and resist insect pests. Good drainage is important, otherwise no bother. Zones 3–9. Height 4 to 5 feet.

Two other plants you might want to investigate:

RUSSIAN SAGE *(Perovskia atriplicifolia)*. A member of the mint family Labiatae that blooms in hot and dry spots. Zones 3–9. Height 3 feet.

BLUE SPIRES *(Caryopteris clandonensis)*. Its flowers are as the name implies—blue. A pretty and underused plant. Zones 5–9. Height 2 feet.

Both of these are hardy and available from White Flower Farm.

All the above-listed plants, except abelia, share a common trait: they are slow to revive in the spring. Don't be impatient with their slowness and give up too soon. Chances are they will put out leaves when they feel like it.

Reminders

☐ Now is the time to buy that traditional fall flower, the chrysanthemum. The freshest pots are in the garden centers, and this is a good week to buy them for spots in the garden that seem "tired." It's best to decide whether you want to go with the "harvest" colors of yellow and rust or pick shades of pink because it's sometimes tough to mix them. Of course, white is a good compromise. I bought some white daisy mums this year myself. Not only do I prefer their flowers, but they have looser growth habits and tend to blend well with plants that have been growing all season, so the effect is more natural. If you want the big decorative chrysanthemums, it is best to grow them in the cutting garden, where an armload can be picked without making a dent in a border. Another advantage to this is that various riotous colors can be mixed without jarring your domestic landscape.

There is a certain amount of disagreement about whether or not it is possible to bring chrysanthemums through the winter and have them bloom well year after year. I'm referring to the more exotic varieties. Many of these aren't fully winter-hardy, and die despite efforts to save them. To avoid being disappointed, if you have a coldframe, store them there for safekeeping and for cuttings in the spring.

☐ Look for other sale items while you are at the garden center. Now is when centers usually reduce their "hard goods" (flowerpots, cachepots, potting soil, tools, and the like). It is also a time to think of containers for bulbs especially if you like to give preplanted narcissus or amaryllis bulbs as Christmas presents. (And gardeners themselves are often happy to receive tools as gifts.)

Confusion exists about the "correct" name for this wonderful annual. Some call it Eustoma grandiflorum; *others refer to it by its old name,* Lisianthus. *Leave the name calling to the experts—buy it when you find it. It is much sturdier than it looks and lasts quite a long time in the garden and when cut.*

Both globe thistle (Echinops humilis 'Taplow Blue'), *Zones 4–9, and sea holly* (Eryngium maritimum), *Zones 3–7, need to be grown in poor soil in good, strong sun. They have very interesting blue stems and leaves and dry very well.*

Giant sunflowers

Medium yellow sunflowers with brown eyes

Mixed sunflowers

Italian white sunflowers

The Last
Week of
August

The Last Week of August

The sky was suddenly filled with swallows this week—a sure sign that fall is around the corner. They travel and fly in great flocks, turning and swirling together. Reeds down by the water's edge are now dark with plumelike flowers, and must also be dense with bugs, because that seems to be the birds' favorite spot in late afternoon. They remain there chirping and feeding until dark, then get back to work with the first light of dawn. I don't know how they spend their days. Probably waiting patiently on phone wires.

Many of the roses are into their late bloom now. They are always a treat. The *Rosa rugosa* is also covered with bright red hips—a pretty sight. These brightly colored little "apples" are also good to use in bouquets.

I started clearing out some of the beds in earnest this week. Many things will be maturing and dying back soon. Some gardeners like to do rather extensive filling in with nursery-grown blooming plants, but I never do this, except with a few white chrysanthemums, because I don't mind the look of beds with just a few sturdy last plants in flower surrounded by neatly manicured open spaces. This is when a mulch covering is really important. Of course, perennials will—just like the roses—give a second modest blooming.

My sweet autumn clematis *(Clematis paniculata)* is filled with buds. Probably will get that first rush of white flowers and splendid fragrance by next week. I've mentioned this vine before, but be reminded. It grows fast, 30 feet a year, so you can run it up an old tree or use it to disguise something ugly. As with all clematis, its flowers are followed by pretty swirls of seed heads.

Another plant that I put into my cutting garden that is extremely fragrant is Mexican tuberose. It is also full of buds. These flowers must be planted each year, just like gladiolus. The single variety is my choice to use in bouquets, although the doubles seem more popular. Their scent is too overpowering for some people, but I like it.

Reminders

☐ If you have been growing geraniums and plan to keep them, you can soon start getting them ready to move inside for the winter. The trick here is to make sure there is plenty of sun where they are placed. They like to be close to the windowpane. One year I had two rows of 6-inch pots at a south window and the ones in front did all the blooming. But in general they are most satisfactory winter bloomers. Before bringing geraniums in, trim them back severely and give them a helping of fertilizer. The growth that they put out during the winter will be no good when they move back outside next summer. So the process will have to be repeated—trimming, but sparingly fertilized this time. Going to the bother of wintering geraniums over is doubly important if you have a plant whose color you especially like. You can't always count on finding these odd colors every year.

☐ Start harvesting any herbs you're growing in with the flowers. Now is when they get somewhat overgrown. Hang bundles of herbs just as you do the flowers in the "How to Dry Flowers" section, see page 125. Of all the herbs, I have had most success with digging and wintering over rosemary plants. They have a nice shape, which they will retain all during their stay inside, if you have sufficient sun and don't overwater and overfertilize.

☐ Toward the end of August, the garden centers usually begin getting a fresh supply of foliage plants, as well as fall bloomers like gloxinia. Take a look before they have gotten picked over.

☐ Take a look at your lawn. If it looks less than wonderful and requires only a small job of patching and revitalizing, you can probably do it yourself. But if the lawn is really in bad shape, call in a professional and discuss the job. Lawn work can cost like the devil, so be prepared. However, if you think you can handle it by yourself without outside help, here are some tips:

Start off by killing crabgrass and weeds with special weed killer. If you are an organic gardener, dig up the weeds with a pointed digger. (Don't dispose of them on the compost heap.)

Next, rake with a bamboo or plastic rake. You want to get all debris and dead grass out of the lawn. If the dead grass is really thick, you may need to rent a thatching machine, which can do the job very quickly—so the rental won't be too bad.

When you go for grass seed to replant the barren areas, be sure to get a good blend that suits the particular spot you need to cover. Grass seeds come in various mixtures, some of which contain a lot of quick-start ryegrass seed and less of the finer-textured bluegrass and red fescue. Read labels carefully before you decide. Your seed salesman should be of some help, if you display a bit of knowledge yourself. Note: be wary of clover. It makes a dense spreading mat, but, if not frequently mowed, produces lots of flowers.

After you have got everything ready for planting and the soil in the bald spots loosened and smoothed, set up a temporary irrigation system to keep the new grass seed moist as it germinates. Seeds need warm (not hot) days and cool nights for germination. If the seeds germinate and then are allowed to dry out, all is lost. You will have to start all over again. So, as is almost always the case when starting any plants, water is the key. Plan accordingly.

It's a good idea to lime your lawn in the fall so that the lime can begin to have some effect neutralizing soil that is too acid. Do not let it drift into areas where you grow rhododendrons, azaleas, or heathers—they hate it and will probably show their wrath by letting some of their branches wither and die on you.

Fertilize your lawn every other year in the fall, too. It will have a chance to take effect during the winter also—as soil shifts and moves about during the periods of freezing and thawing.

These giant sunflowers (Helianthus) are called 'Mammoth' by Burpee. They should be grown in full sun and be protected from the wind (hard to do). They can grow to a height of almost 10 feet, which makes them really out of scale almost everyplace except in the distance. Annual.

These medium-sized sunflowers (Helianthus) are like the 'Autumn Beauties' except that they are all yellow. Annual, height 4 feet.

This mixture of variegated sunflowers (Helianthus) is called 'Autumn Beauty.' They come in a wonderful range of brown, mahogany, and yellow combinations. Flowers are about medium-sized. Annuals, 4 feet.

Although these are called 'Italian White' sunflowers (Helianthus), they obviously are just a more refined yellow than their sometime giant cousins. These last very well when cut (early in the morning) and will do best if popped into warm water with most of their lower leaves removed. Annual, 4 feet.

How to Dry Flowers

How to Dry Flowers

There are essentially two methods of preserving flowers to use in bouquets. One is by hanging them until they dry, and the other is by immersing the flower in some sort of medium that will draw out moisture, leaving color and shape more or less intact. Pressing distorts form, and the use of glycerine doesn't work too well on flowers, because it turns them dark. But it is fine for leaves.

Obviously, the easiest method is to dry by hanging, and that is the only one I have ever attempted. Interestingly enough, many of the basic cautions for making "dry" potpourri apply here. As with that method, you will have to find a well-ventilated spot where the humidity and light can be controlled or are fairly consistent. This may sound as if it will be a bother, but that isn't necessarily so. For instance, plants hung under a stairwell would work if it is not sunny or exposed there. Or in an attic with rafters, where the air moves freely. Kitchens and bathrooms are no good because of the humidity. Stillness and humidity can promote mildew and mold. And lack of heat can mean flowers will not dry quickly enough to preserve their color. If you are serious about this, it might be a good idea to invest in an inexpensive hydrometer to measure humidity—which should be between 40 and 50 percent. And since the way to correct too much humidity is by the use of heat, the ideal spot is an unused (or seldom used) studio or bedroom where correcting humidity would not be a great inconvenience. The truth is you never quite know where the best spot in the house (or garage) will be, so the first time you try this, hang bunches of the same flower in a number of places and see how they work out. After a week, you will be able to tell the difference in locations.

When you have found the right spot and selected the flowers (more on that later), divide them into small bundles after removing the bottom leaves and one or two around the flower itself. Place the heads so that they are not mashed together and cut stems off to the same length. Tie each bunch carefully and leave a loop on the end to hang it by. After tying with string, wrap the ends with a rubber band. This is a precaution, because as the stems dry, they shrink. And if you don't have a chance to check them often to make sure they are secure, they might slip out of their string noose.

You want the bunches to be small, because with larger ones flowers in the center don't have the air circulation to prevent mildew. Also, crowding blossoms together can press them out of shape. That's about all there is to it. Of course, results will vary from year to year. Sometimes the weather is uncooperative, which affects drying conditions and the quality and moisture content of the flowers themselves.

Many grasses and seed heads can be dried flat on brown paper, while other flowers with large heads that partially dry on their own stem, like hydrangea, can be left upright.

Obviously, some plants dry more successfully than others, but almost any flower can be preserved by some method. However, things like delphinium (which is beautiful when properly dried) require a bit of technique, which you acquire with experience. Still and all, there are many to start on that are practically foolproof and give you satisfying results. A partial list of the easiest includes statice, yarrow, strawflower, baby's breath, globe thistle, heather, Chinese lantern, goldenrod, and, of course, roses and hydrangeas.

Flowers should be picked when the air is dry and when there is no moisture on their petals or leaves. In the case of roses, you get the best results if they are picked in bud, just as the first petals are beginning to open. Leaves and flowers will shrivel somewhat, but they will still be pretty. Roses may also be dried flat. Their color will darken as they dry, so the reds are not always the best to select. A color in the medium range is better.

For hydrangeas, always choose flower heads that are mature and have turned leathery (but still have their color). You may dry these by hanging or by laying them flat, but the latter choice can result in distorted shape. They may also be left with their stems in a small amount of water (in a vase that will hold them loosely). The water then is allowed to evaporate gradually.

As to the second method—using a drying medium—fine sand is an old choice, which requires that you first prepare the sand by washing and sieving, and then thoroughly drying, either in sunlight or in the oven. After the sand is ready, carefully pour it in around the flowers, which have been placed in a plastic box (cardboard absorbs too much moisture), and leave until the sand does its work. A more modern way is to use commercial silica gel, available at florist supply houses, hobby shops, and sometimes drugstores. But many people still swear by sand. Once flowers are dry, they must be carefully removed and brushed lightly to get rid of grains that may be clinging to them. These will usually have to be wired to a stem. I don't really know enough about all of this to tell you more. For drying by this method, I think you should look at a reference book. A very good one is called, appropriately enough, *The Dried Flower Book,* by Annette Mierhof, with charming illustrations by Marijke den Boer-Vlamings. In this book you will also be told how to use glycerine to preserve leaves and grasses. But before you even make this small investment, give the hang-dry method a try, to be sure you are really interested enough to go on with it.

One last caution: the enemies of the drying process, humidity and strong sunlight, are also the enemies of the dried flower. So keep that in mind when selecting a location for the finished bouquet.

SEPTEMBER

Overleaf: *The pink afternoon light shimmers on water reeds that are filled with birds*

SEPTEMBER

For the first few summers after I built my house, twenty years ago, I had to rent it out for several weeks each year to help meet mortgage payments and to pay for upkeep. I learned very quickly that no matter what, I had to be back in it for Labor Day weekend. This was not so much because I am devoted to the holiday itself, as that Labor Day somehow truly marks the end of summer. Be it early or late according to the calendar, the week after—as if some cosmic lever has been thrown—the sun looks different. And you can feel the slight tilt toward autumn. It may be just as warm as it was the previous week, but the season is over. Geese and small black ducks appear on the pond at twilight, and the moon coming up over it is almost too big and too orange to believe, making its path of light across the dark water directly toward the house. My feelings about this shift are mixed. On the one hand, it is sad for the garden to have to be put to sleep, but at the same time I am ready for it. Except for the four or five crisp weekends in fall, the city is the place for me now. I want to move on like the birds crankily taking off with the first light to complete another leg of their journey. The long trip south.

I recall several years ago, sitting in an old beat-up Jeep, its top down, shaded by a bougainvillea vine that had gotten entangled with a great old light pink oleander— also in bloom. A friend and I were eating ice cream cones, purchased from the outdoor vendor, tucked under all this colorful overhanging splendor. It was February and we had come down to the island of St. Barths in the Caribbean to escape the snow that our friends back home were trudging through at that very moment. No matter that by now daffodils in Bridgehampton were already bravely putting the tips of their leaves up to test the weather. What both the daffodils and I wanted was still months away. Anyway, I was talking about how I wished

I could grow oleander out on Long Island; it was in full flower all around us. Then my friend, who is also an avid gardener, allowed as how she wasn't so sure she would garden at all if she lived in a place that really had no seasons except rainy and dry. I've thought about her remark a number of times since and have decided I probably feel the same. My desire to leave the garden, to put it to sleep for a few months and follow other enthusiasms, is almost as strong in the fall as the opposite is true in the spring. By October's end, you have seen the full cycle. There is nothing left to look forward to but the bleak subtlety of winter, the charm of which eludes me.

But in the meantime there are still wonderful, sometimes the best, days to enjoy, and the very rewarding task of getting ready for winter and the spring to follow. And I need the time out to rekindle my interest. These tasks I tell you about this month can be stretched out over the next two months—or a bit more. The important thing is for you to wind down and bed down the garden properly. Your reward, like planting bulbs, lies ahead, and the procedure can sometimes seem like drudgery unless you come to realize just how much work you can save yourself later by being meticulous now.

I remember one year I had ordered so many daffodil bulbs that I was very late getting them all in—still out planting when it started to snow lightly. (A freaky late-October weather aberration.) I had on a pair of old wool gloves, the fingertips of which had long since given out, and I could feel the cold earth through them. I was cursing for the work I had given myself, when I would much rather have been sitting in front of the fire reading. But I went doggedly ahead. I kept thinking, "What am I doing this for?" but I somehow managed to get through it. And the following spring I got the answer to that question I had put to myself.

A pair of showy dahlias

The humble Joe-Pye weed and a glamorous variety of geranium

A pitcher of strawflowers

A small bouquet of daisy chrysanthemums

Mixed stocks

The common rose mallow

A little bouquet of nasturtiums

The First Week of September

The First Week of September

I don't grow dahlias every year myself. This is probably because I don't like to have to dig them up in the fall and then feel rather guilty about leaving them in the ground, where I know they won't survive the winter. A rather baroque worry. Whatever, if you like dahlias, this is their month. And the coolish nights seem to suit them.

As a matter of fact, you will notice that many flowers besides dahlias take on a more intense and richer color now. As the sun loses some of its strength and the heat ceases to be so relentless, color seems to have more staying power.

I was visiting a friend's garden a couple of days ago and saw that some of his delphiniums were putting out smaller second flowers. These often have oddly shaped stems, which can be very pretty in mixed bouquets. It is amazing how many plants will give you a second blooming about this time—always modest, but a nice little farewell to the season.

September is a good month to take stock of your garden and to decide what you do and don't like about the way it worked out this season. Were you satisfied with the placement of plants? Did the heights work out? How were the color combinations? Did you go through too long a period without color in a spot that needed it? If, for any reason, you are dissatisfied and want to change your beds and borders, here is a simple plan of action.

First, it helps to make a rough sketch of the garden (in plan form) and then mark where you want to move certain plants. It's easy to forget once you find yourself outside and actually doing the job.

Next, for two or three days before the move, water (well) those plants slated to be transplanted and trim off extra-long growth. This will minimize the trauma of the move. And try to do this moving on an overcast day—certainly not at high noon. If you are unable to wait for clouds, do it late in the afternoon.

Dig the hole before you dig the plant, so it won't have to be out of the ground too long. If, on the other hand, you are not sure where to put it, stash it in a plastic pot (from the garden center) and try it in various locations until it looks at home. A plastic pot is lightweight and will keep the dirt from falling away from the roots. Should it not be placed in the ground right away, let the plant rest in the shade, and be sure it is kept well sprinkled while you are making up your mind.

When doing the actual planting, add water to the hole first and fill in with good soil or compost, if you have it. Don't use poor clay or sand; give your plant a good start. And don't fertilize. All it will need is plenty of water.

Label the transplant, if possible, because it can be hard to remember what you have planted (and where) by the time next year rolls around. Trim off any leaves or flowers that were damaged during the moving. Many gardeners remove all flowers and about a quarter of the foliage so the plant will put a large portion of its strength into new roots. Once it is settled, keep an eye on the plant over the next weeks for signs of wilting. Come to the rescue with water, should this occur. Some wilting is OK, but a totally wilted plant should be cut back to about 4 inches and allowed to rest. Don't give up. The plant will likely be fine next spring. And don't let weeds get started around its base.

A word about mulching. Put the mulch around, not on top of, the plant. The point is to keep the ground a steady temperature, not to keep the plant warm. And although you probably don't want to think of frost now, when cold weather has knocked out the bulk of your perennials, cut them off to about 2 or 3 inches. The purpose of leaving this bit of stem is to keep the mulch from packing down on top of the plant's crown, which could cause it to rot. Air circulation is important. Obviously, while you are doing this pruning you should dig out and discard any plant that is in poor shape. And have an eye peeled for grubs and other pests. Keep the area clean. Garden litter is one of their favorite nesting places.

Late next month you should dig your dahlia and gladiolus bulbs. Do this carefully with a garden fork so as not to damage any. Clean dirt off and label them for color. They can be stored in a cool cellar. Ideally, the temperature should hover around fifty degrees Fahrenheit and be no more than sixty. Some people put their bulbs in sand, but I don't think that is necessary. They will be fine if they are not packed in together too tightly and the temperature doesn't get out of hand for too long a period.

As the season progresses and the ground gets harder, you may want to scatter some seeds for early-starting plants next spring. Plants that can be treated this way are poppies (both California and Iceland), larkspurs, and forget-me-nots. In fact, any seeds sold as "early-planting" can be risked with fall planting, except in the far north, where it's too cold too early.

Roses need special mulching attention, as some of them are very tender and cannot tolerate long periods of really freezing weather. In most places you can usually get away with piling compost or well-rotted manure around the base of the bushes to the height of a foot. If roses are in an exposed area and are very tender, you should erect a burlap screen around them. To my way of thinking, it is almost easier to move a bush to a more protected spot than to go to all this trouble each year. Anyway, each area has its special requirements, and if you grow a lot of roses you should investigate local practices.

Now, after the ground is really hard and you have spread whatever mulch you intend to use (in Zone 7 this is after Christmas), you can press leftover tree branches into use as winter protection. If you live in a windy place without much snow, you may have to anchor the branches with stakes pushed into the earth at an angle to keep everything from blowing away. I know all this must sound like a lot of bother, but by a little experimenting you will quickly learn just how much (or how little) you have to do to make it through to spring.

Last, snow is the best mulch of all, and when your plants are blanketed by a deep layer of it, you probably have nothing to worry about.

There isn't very much I can tell you about these bold dahlias, because they were given to me by someone who had had the tubers for so many years that she couldn't remember what they were. Growing along in the same row were others that were much whiter, so probably these are a sport.

The red geranium pictured here is called Pelargonium, *'Red Fountain.' Like all geraniums, it benefits from deadheading, so taking a few flowers for a bouquet is OK.* Joe-Pye weed (Eupatorium maculatum) *grows wild from Canada to the Carolinas and across the northern United States. It is partial to damp areas. Lore has it that an Indian called Joe-Pye used it to cure fevers and early American colonists used it to treat typhus.*

This sunflower (Helianthus) *was picked just before the seeds at its center began to mature. Interestingly enough, this particular variety, Burpee's 'Sunbird Hybrid,' is found in the vegetable section of the catalog. This is because it is primarily grown for its seeds, which are good for birds and people. 'Sunbird' is a good type to plant for cutting because it reaches a height of about 6 to 7 feet, making it shorter than most of this size of flower, and it matures in 68 days, as opposed to the more common one called 'Mammoth,' which requires 80 days. When ground is warm, plant in an isolated spot, or its seeds will keep coming up each year and be a nuisance in the "tamer" parts of the garden.*

Strawflowers (Helichrysum) *are annuals and are familiar to many people because they are so often used in dried bouquets. Even when "green" the flowers have a slightly brittle feel. Strawflowers need good strong sunlight to grow in and can reach a height of almost 3 feet although there are some shorter (14-inch) varieties. Incidentally, if you dry them, pick bouquets of flowers before they are fully opened and hang them upside down. See "How to Dry Flowers," page 126.*

I'm particularly fond of small-flowered daisy mums. This particular variety is called 'Daisy White' and can be bought from White Flower Farm. However, these and similar varieties are often available at local nurseries in the fall. These should really be replaced now and then, even though they are considered perennial—they tend to run out of steam after a few years. Daisy mums are also more likely to blend in with the garden because of their loose form. Zones 5–10.

These flowers (Hibiscus moscheutos) *often grow wild in marshy areas and can stand brackish water. I have some pink ones that turned up by my pond's edge several years ago. The particular one pictured is called 'Southern Belle.' They grow to a height of 3 to 4 feet. Zones 5–10.*

After placing a container in the basket to hold water, I cut the stems of the stocks (Matthiola) *to the desired length and put them in all at the same time. This way they don't flop around as you are trying to arrange them. The ones here are the dwarf variety (12 to 18 inches), which is hardier and less demanding than its taller relative (2½ feet). Both are annuals.*

Nasturtiums (Tropacolum) *are annuals and the seeds should be planted when the ground is warm. They germinate very quickly then. You should try to plant them in the spot where you want them to be, because they don't much like being transplanted. Nowadays, you have several kinds to choose from. For sprawl there is 'Semi-Tall Double Gleam.' For a tidy small plant select 'Double Dwarf Jewel.' For climbing, 'Fordhook Favorite.' Personally, I prefer the old-fashioned single variety.*

A bouquet of "quilled" chrysanthemums

Dahlias, cockscombs, and wild sunflowers

Goldenrod, giant reed, and wild grasses

The Second Week of September

A mixed bunch of fall dahlias

The Second Week of September

I had a look at my garden diary, comparing the last few years, and I see that this week is often a throwback to summer. It certainly is this time around. However, I don't fall for it—I know what is in the cards—so I just enjoy the bonus warmth and go about the job of winding down.

As the perennials finish their blooming and the flower heads mature, we cut them back to within 4 to 5 inches of the ground. This will not only neaten the beds, but is good for them.

I ordered six 'Raubritter' roses last week (see June's opening photograph). If you want special roses for next year, they should be ordered now. Many nurseries have limited stock of the more unusual or popular varieties and will be out of them if you wait until after the first of the year. Arrange for bushes to be shipped to arrive as soon as the danger of frost is over. In my case, that is April 15.

Between this week and the end of the month, try to check shrubs and smaller plants for infestations. Since one of my great pleasures is inspecting plants to see how they are doing, this is no inconvenience for me. But if you aren't in the habit of doing as I do, get to it. And pull off dead iris leaves. If they look eaten or diseased, they should be burned, to avoid spreading infections.

I notice my local nurseries have gotten a lot of evergreen stock in for fall planting. Evergreens are an extremely important part of the garden, providing the background to build in front of, and around. They also help to keep the garden from looking so forbidding in winter. This is an extensive subject that I have not really devoted much space to—so now is the time.

What follows is a brief listing of some possibilities. This is only a starter. When you have time, read a little more in a reference book and then go to the nurseries to have a look at the real thing. Evergreens usually are planted for the life of the garden and are slower to mature than many other plants. So you can see how important it is to have a little knowledge before investing.

The following list of trees and plants is divided according to size, because the range is so broad. All like sun. Tallest first: Engelmann's spruce, 150 feet. This is preferable to the more common Colorado blue spruce, 100 feet. Both, Zones 2–3 to 7. Norway spruce, 150 feet, is good but overused, and loses branches at the base, although it is fast-growing. Zones 3–7. Serbian spruce, 100 feet, is considered one of the best. Zones 4–7.

Then there are the pines. Eastern white pine, to 150 feet. Able to withstand some shade as well as create it. Japanese white pine, 50 feet. Has a wide and elegant form with a bluish cast to its needles. Zones 5–8. Japanese black pine, 130 feet. Good for tough sites near the shore. In some areas it has fallen victim to both borers and tip moths. Check this out first. Zones 4–7.

A related genus of trees is the firs. These do not do well where summers are extremely hot and dry, but are listed as being hardy in Zones 3–4 to 7. The white fir, 120 feet, is a good tree and has the same bluish tone as the overused blue spruce, but is much softer in the landscape. Zones 4–6. These trees must never be topped, because a large part of their beauty is in their symmetry (if that is what you like).

Other sun-loving tall trees include eastern red cedar, 75 feet. A long-lived narrow tree in varying shades of green through silver. Incidentally, junipers shouldn't be planted close to apple or crab apple, since they are an alternate host for apple rust. But they are tough and robust and able to withstand drought and generally poor conditions. Zones 2–8.

Don't overlook hollies. Although they are slow-growing, they can be lovely in the garden. They may be a hedge or a specimen on the lawn. English holly, 50 feet (in the U.S.). Zones 6–7 to 8–9. American holly, 50 feet. Foliage is less glossy than the English, but has fine bright berries and can stand a hard winter. Zones 5–9. There are new hybrids on the market, so ask your nurseryman for advice.

Many people think of the old standby American arborvitae, 60 feet, as the answer to all screening problems. It is awfully overused, but is strong and pest-resistant. Zones 2–8. Probably the aristocrat of screening is the common English yew, 60 feet. Yews vary in hardiness. However, they not only screen but give a good strong background. They also have another good quality, in that their root systems go very deep. This means they do not compete for nutrients with the borders around them, the way privet does, for instance. This is an extremely large and varied genus of plants, so go to a nursery and look at them.

In the shady areas of your property, useful evergreens include hemlocks, 75 to 90 feet. Zones 3–5. These easily transplanted trees should not be sheared, as some people do. Trim back by pruning selectively.

One last suggestion for special situations: the true cedars. Look at Atlas blue cedar and the somewhat stiffer relative Deodar cedar. Both grow to 120 to 150 feet and are hardy in Zones 6–7 to 9. These need to be isolated and enjoyed on their own in an open area.

Now for middle-size evergreens. Two excellent ones are Swiss stone pine, 75 feet, Zones 3–7 (slow-growing), and Hinoki false cypress, 15 feet, Zones 3–8.

Low-growing evergreens include most rhododendrons and camellias (although in parts of the South they can grow to 30 feet)—and some of the following, which will add a bit of character all year round to the garden: prostrate Norway spruce, 3 feet. Zones 3–8. Bird's nest spruce, 5 feet. Zones 2–8. Dwarf Alberta spruce, 12 feet. Zones 3–7. For dwarf junipers, those labeled Nana stay truly small. Some of the best are Shore juniper, 1 foot. Zones 5–8. Parson's juniper, 3 feet. Zones 5–8. Creeping juniper, 18 inches. Zones 2–8. ('Bar Harbor' is a wonderfully blue and beautiful variety of this plant.) And there is a golden shrub of greater height called 'Pfitzerana Gold Star,' 5 feet high—with a spread of 6 feet. Zones 3–8.

Japanese skimmia, 5 feet, looks like a member of the holly family. Zones 6–8. Boxwood is evergreen in areas where winters are not too severe. English or common boxwood, 2 feet. Zones 6–9. Korean and Japanese boxwood are tougher. And 'Kingsville Dwarf' is one of the best there is, 1 foot high and sometimes 3 feet across. Zones 5–8.

Most evergreens mentioned here are sturdy and able to flourish on their own once they have been pampered through their first year of growth. Keep an eye on the low-growing kinds for spider mites and similar pests, especially in unusually hot weather and around terraces or in other hot spots where the heat is reflected and multiplied. A strong spray with the hose every other day can forestall problems. Also, keeping the leaves washed enables them to breathe better and promotes robust health.

A word of caution: be careful when you mix the blues and greens of the evergreen world. Often they don't. But you can slide from one color to the other by using divider plants of a more neutral "true green."

If you decide to do the trick of using a live Christmas tree and then planting it, dig the hole for it in October, before the ground freezes. Fill the hole with straw and cover it with burlap. Keep the tree moist (but not soaked) while in the house. After the holiday, move it to the garage for several days, where it will be cold but not frozen. This will help it to adapt to being outside again.

These "quilled" mums are also sometimes referred to as 'Spider' mums. They grow to a height of 18 inches and like sun, although they can stand a bit of shade. Many people replace mums every year because they don't like the way they look after the lower leaves brown off and die. If you would like to replace yours, take cuttings and keep pinching them back until July to give them a bushy shape. Zones 4–10.

Included here are dahlias, possibly similar to one from Scheeper's called 'House of Orange'—a steady bloomer—and a mixture of interesting colors of small cockscombs (Celosia) of the "plume" variety. The yellow flower is a variety of Helianthus, therefore related to the sunflower.

Did you know that goldenrod (Solidago rugosa), which grows almost all over the United States, is a highly valued ornamental in England and that Henry VIII supposedly planted it at Hampton Court? I thought not. Seen here with giant reed (Phragmites communis) and various wild grasses. Incidentally, Phragmites is what you see covering the giant Hackensack meadows just before you cross into New York City from New Jersey.

I really don't know what varieties these are, because they were given to me by a friend. But good "named" dahlias are getting harder and harder to find. The rarer ones are saved from year to year, and the best way to get them is to ask a generous grower for a spare. Included in this mix may be a relative of 'Edinburgh,' bicolored, 'Gerrie Hoek,' an excellent pinky orange. The red one at the center may be 'Arabian Night.'

Globe amaranth

Two kinds of late-blooming hydrangeas

Dried blue hydrangeas

The Third Week of September

A basket of marigolds

Roses and weeds

The Third Week of September

The cool nights have continued, and how wonderfully clear the air is now. What a treat after the haze of August. Makes the color of vegetation and the water in the distance almost unreal. Especially at the end of the day.

The other afternoon I saw a beautiful sourwood plant covered with red leaves. It really is a medium-size tree, which grows to about 60 feet. I understand they usually have white spikelike clusters on them about now, but this one didn't have many. I think I'll put one in if I can find the space. Almost every plant I have chosen in the last few years was selected in just this way. I'll see something in someone's garden or stumble across it at a nursery. I know this isn't really the best method—particularly since I seem to be so hellbent on careful planning. But in the long run it all evens out. At least I plant things I like, rather than what I'm told to. This reminds me of conversations I had with one of the oldest and most established nurserymen in the area when I first built my house and was taking tentative steps in landscaping (on a tight budget). He gave me some very good advice—among the things he suggested was that I buy all those black pine seedlings, which are now large trees surrounding the property. He was also one of the most negative fellows I have ever come across. Almost everything I had my heart set on growing, he rather gleefully (I imagined) told me wouldn't grow "out where you are." Like most natives of the area, he thought we were all crazy to want to be perched within reach of the ocean's dampness and fog. "Too windy. Too sandy." "Salt air'll kill it." Of course, he was right about some things—but not about everything. These little talks left me so frustrated that I wound up planting everything. This reminds me of something Dorothy Parker was supposed to have said: "When someone says to you 'I'm going to tell you this for your own good,' run for the hills." Anyway, I was pleasantly surprised at what did survive—and then thrive. A piece of land does not have the same exposures or temperature over its whole expanse. So if something doesn't work in one part of your garden, it might well like it in another spot. And the only way you will know is to give it a try. I learned some very good things about gardening in general from the old veteran, but I also learned from him that no one (that we are likely to come in contact with, anyway) can tell you for sure. Finally you are left on your own. So if there is anything to be learned from this long-winded anecdote about my early gardening experience, it is "plunge ahead."

In August I promised to tell you when you should gather the heads of black-eyed Susans to naturalize. It is now. Probably too late for wild daisies, though.

While you have the clippers out, look at the roses. Often they have put out a great deal of long growth by this time. If a bush is in a windy spot, you had best trim it to keep it from being caught in the wind; swaying around too much could loosen the roots. As roses end their blooming, hill up earth, old manure, or compost around them, covering the base of the plant to about 8 inches. If you live in a colder climate, even more protection might be needed—in the form of more mulch and even a burlap screen if plants are situated in a particularly vulnerable area. Pampered roses give you awfully nice rewards the following season.

On one of your tours of the garden, look at more than the plants. Check for loose bricks on the terrace, leaky faucets, shaky gutters, and unstable trellises. When you need repair work done, the fall is the time to start lining up workers for the job. If where you live is anything like here, you have a devil of a time in the spring trying to get any of these odd jobs finished—sometimes even just getting anyone to look at them at all.

If you have trees close to the house and there are dead branches—or dangerously overhanging ones—have them taken care of before the winter storms do it for you. A big branch falling across the roof can do plenty of damage.

The following are things that you might want to keep in mind for between now and the time everything starts to freeze. They are odd jobs and have no particular priority:

As life in the garden begins to wind down, empty planters and pots that have fulfilled their purpose for the year. Put clay pots where they won't freeze—or they will crack. Get hoses emptied and coiled, so they won't freeze. And if yours is a summer house, which you plan to close for the season, you will not be doing birds a favor by feeding them. This should be done only if you plan to keep it up all winter. They quickly learn to depend on man's kindness, so it is difficult for them when it is withdrawn.

After the foliage on gladioluses has matured, dig them up and shake off excess dirt and store the corms. Do the same with dahlias. Label these, at least according to color, so you will know what you are doing next spring.

Set up a work space inside for potting up herbs that you want to keep growing in the house. Even newspaper spread out on a counter near the sink will do. When you are finished, simply fold the rubbish into a package and heave it into the trash. This avoids getting dirt in the sink and all over everything.

As you start bringing in plants for the winter, check under the leaves for infestations. Any that are too far gone, and can't be cured or cleaned by the time they must be brought in, should be gotten rid of. You must be firm about this. Diseased plants can ruin your whole inside garden. In the closed-in atmosphere of the house, infections spread like measles used to in kindergarten.

If you are planning to prune any trees or shrubs in the fall, you must be sure that they have gone dormant before you do so. Otherwise, the pruning will trigger new growth, which will only be killed off by the cold and weaken the whole plant. If you are in doubt about a particular species, look it up in a garden reference book.

Speaking of books, I hope you have been keeping up with your garden diary. This can sometimes be tedious, but simple notations about the beginnings and endings of blooming cycles, weather conditions, and dates of when new plants are put in the garden will do. Note the name of the particular variety, if you know it. Try to do this weekly. It takes only a few minutes and can be very helpful next year—or years from now.

Finally, when everything is safely done, take time to care for your tools. Oil them so they won't rust or corrode during the winter. Even sharpen them (or have them sharpened) now, if you have the time.

You don't have to do all these things. But any one of the chores done in the fall will make things run smoother in the spring—which isn't too far away if you start watching for signs in a few months.

Globe amaranth (Gomphrena globosa) is a tough little annual that grows to a height of 18 to 24 inches. Many people mistake it for clover, the flowers of which it resembles. Grow it in pots or out-of-doors, but make sure it is in a warm, or even hot, place and that it is dry.

The long-pointed white hydrangea (H. paniculata) is called 'Grandiflora.' Its flowers resemble wisteria. Zones 3–8. Although this plant can grow to a height of almost 20 feet, it is best kept low because it doesn't look too good in the winter. The heads of greenish hydrangeas are actually white ones that change to this very pretty color as they mature. I let this bouquet dry in the vase and the flowers kept their shape very well, although the 'Grandiflora' took on a tan cast.

These are dried old-fashioned blue hydrangeas (Hydrangea macrophylla 'All Summer Beauty'). They dry very nicely and retain just enough of their original color to make a beautiful bouquet. Hydrangeas are hardy in Zones 7–9, but should be protected with mulch around the base in exposed areas. The plant from which these flowers were taken generally grows to a height of 3 to 4 feet.

I don't recall what the name of this old climbing rose is, and all efforts to get a positive identification failed; I gave up after I got four different names from four different knowledgeable sources. Whatever it is, it is hardy and blooms all summer and well into the fall, stopping only when the frost gets it. The brown weed is dock (Rumex). For something that turns such a gorgeous color when it goes to seed, it is a terrible garden pest. Mainly this is due to the fact that it has a very long taproot that is difficult to get out.

These marigolds are Burpee's 'Yellow Nugget,' which grow to about 12 inches, producing flowers about 2 inches in diameter. I don't mind the odor of marigolds, but if you do, Burpee has developed an "odorless" one.

These are among the simplest flowers to grow and are very good for children's gardens (and are more fun than radishes). Organically minded gardeners say that marigolds help to keep the garden free of nematodes.

The Last Week of September

The Last Week of September

T his has been one of those half-and-half weeks, when the weather can seem like midsummer, and then deny it by presenting you with a crystal-clear, cool morning that unmistakably says fall. We are in the changes. Many plants have hardened off and are ready for what they know is ahead, and I just pulled out the last of the annuals in the cutting garden—a few hardy and tenacious yellow marigolds. I then raked it over in preparation for its quiet period. Doing this gave me a great deal of pleasure—seeing it cleaned and ready for its winter coating of hay. The dozen or so rosebushes planted around the cutting garden's edge are all still sending out a few flowers. They stop only when the frost tells them it's time to quit.

As I was walking back to the house I heard wild geese honking overhead.

If you are interested in making a cutting garden for yourself, now is the time to plan (and plant some of it). The same caution I gave about the garden in general applies to the cutting garden. That is, don't make it too big. An area 15 feet square is enough. You can get lots of plants into something this size and still be able to keep it looking fairly good in hot weather. The most common mistake beginners seem to make is locking themselves into an oversized garden, which then looks terrible and discourages them permanently.

But first things first. And the first thing is, where? If you can manage it, choose a location with full sun most of the day, capable of being partially screened from view. Remember, this is for cutting, not looking—although it will thrive best if kept clean. But the truth is, plants that have been cut back to get the flowers don't look especially nice. This spot should also be where you can get a hose to it easily. When you get around to the watering stage next year, remember to investigate soakers that can be attached to the faucet with a timer. Anyway, this is a working garden and may be used not only for cut flowers, but as a testing bed for plants from the nursery that you don't know much about or whose general growing requirements are still unknown to you. I also reserve a small part of my garden for growing a few annuals to slip into my perennial beds as needed. I don't usually grow these from seed, but rather from plants that I buy at the nursery. If grown from seed, they should be started in the house or in a coldframe. Bedding plants that I like are white snapdragons, pink verbenas and pink and white eustomas. Or anything that has a long blooming period and is easy to transplant. And last, sadly, sometimes this is an infirmary for plants you want to nurse back to health, which have been furloughed from their permanent spot. It may also do double duty as an herb or salad garden.

You will probably want to fence it somehow. (However, it is easiest to rototill the space before fencing.) And always add aged manure, compost, and fertilizer at the very beginning, so that all plants have a chance to start off on their best foot. If rabbits are a problem—or young children and household pets (yours or otherwise)—you almost have to fence. For rabbits, dig a narrow trench around the area about a foot deep and set the fence at the bottom of the trench. Then fill it in and rabbits can't burrow under. Make sure your fence posts are treated lumber and are set securely in the ground. If the fence is only 2 feet high, you won't need a gate, providing you are reasonably agile. But don't push your luck with higher fences. Gates don't always have to be hinged, either. If you use chicken wire to fence, it too should be buried in the ground.

Now comes the fun part—selecting what you want to grow. Think in rows. Each should be about 2 feet wide, with a path in between about the same, although you could manage with a narrower path. I put down a good covering of mulch to walk on and to keep weeds at bay. Flowers in a cutting garden are like vegetable gardens—you have an overabundance of one thing all at once. Remember, not too many plants are needed to provide flowers for a bouquet, so don't overplant a single variety unless it is something you use in lots of bouquets (in my case this is white, cream, and green zinnias, or any white flower). A sample list would be something like: a hundred tulips in your favorite colors (don't forget white ones for balance). It takes about two dozen flowers to make a decent bouquet. Twenty hyacinths for fragrance. Fifty of the rarer narcissuses, like pink-cupped Salome or the exotic collar daffodils. Twenty lilies that bloom at different times during the summer (not daylilies, which grow well in the beds—and don't make very good cut flowers anyway). Then any combination of annuals that you like. Each year I usually try one I've never grown before.

After earlier daffodils and narcissuses have bloomed, you can dig them up and put them in the wilder area among your naturalized ones, or you can let them die back and interplant with your annuals—zinnias, cleomes, etc. After tulips have bloomed it's best to dig them up and then replace them next fall. If this is too extravagant for you, fertilize them three times—just as they poke out of the ground, while blooming, and afterward as their foliage dies back. (There is more on tulips in the May section.) To plant bulbs, follow the same rules as for planting in the wild (see below). Depth charts are usually in the bulb catalogs.

One last thought before going on to the next thing: if it's possible, try to have a little shed nearby to store tools, fertilizer (must be kept dry), flowerpots, and all the odds and ends of gardening. You might also want to consider a compost heap and coldframe. But I would leave this for a later time. One extra project a year is enough. Think of this area as you would your kitchen, and plan it with care. Right down to a place to sit and rest when you can.

Now to planting bulbs. There are two places for them—in the garden for cutting, as above, and in areas for looking at, such as drifts under trees or naturalized in meadows. Or in perennial beds. Among the bulbs, tulips don't naturalize, and the hybridized varieties of hyacinths look too overblown to appear natural. Wild hyacinths are best for this purpose. Daffodils and narcissuses are the great naturalizers.

Open your bulbs when they arrive and put them in a cool spot. Don't refrigerate them. The smaller bulbs or miniatures should be planted right away so they will have time to make roots before the coldest weather sets in. Larger daffodils can wait a bit, and tulips should be held until late October or into the first weeks of November. Wild hyacinths are included in the "smaller bulb" group.

Now I am going to tell you how the textbooks say you should plant narcissuses and daffodils for naturalizing. Then I'll tell you how I do it.

According to the books, you should remove the sod or grass in an area at least 1 yard square (this should be removed in such a way that it can be replaced to cover the bulbs, and should wait on a tarp or piece of burlap). Dig and cultivate the exposed area and fertilize with bone meal. Drop a handful of bulbs on the prepared bed. Set them securely upright where they fall. This will ensure that the planting has a random look. Then replace the soil carefully on top of the bulbs and water deeply to get them off to a good start. Working this way enables you to manage a large area in a sensible manner, getting in three or four areas a day without breaking your back. If you have them handy, you can also sow a few wildflower seeds at the same time. I must confess I have never done it like this, and am quoting a friend who swears by this method and gets spectacular results to prove it.

My way requires a helper (no prior experience necessary) and a good sharp pointed-end shovel. Drop handfuls of bulbs on the ground first. Then, being careful not to step on or move any, plant them where they have fallen by pushing the shovel all the way into the ground with your foot and then making a slit in the soil by forcing the handle away from you while the blade is still in the ground. Your helper then puts the bulb(s) in the slit, along with bone meal. While he or she holds the bulb in place, pull the shovel out and stamp the ground back down. I've planted hundreds of bulbs this way (narcissuses and daffodils only) and have had marvelous results. I tried one of those little round bulb-planting contraptions, only once. I'd still be planting my first batch if I had gone on with it. An absolutely pointless tool, so far as I'm concerned.

Whatever method you use, don't plant in rows. That is why you drop bulbs on the ground and plant them where they fall. There seems to be an instinctive impulse to line things up. Resist it.

And finally, since we started the book with daffodils, it seems right somehow to be closing it with instructions for planting them to bloom next spring. A full circle has been drawn, with us in the middle. Good luck to us both.

The trumpet-shaped flowers are tube-roses, which come from a bulb and must be planted like gladioluses in zones north of 8. They are rather slow growers, so should be placed in rich soil as soon as the ground is warmed and the danger of frost is over. Supposedly, if planted in mid-May in my zone they will bloom toward the end of August. It never works out that way for me. I almost never get any flowers until the latter part of September. So if you want earlier bloom, I suggest starting them in the house—or a coldframe. Incidentally tuberoses make nice pot plants. They might not be the prettiest, but they sure smell wonderful if you are partial to strong fragrance. Their average height is 30 inches, but in the garden they seldom require staking. Dig the bulbs just before frost and store them in a dry place until next year.

The gray-white spires are salvia (S. farinacea). It, and its more common blue relative are both wonderful in bouquets. The only problem is that their seeds are hard to germinate, requiring about 12 weeks indoors to get going. Salvia is a perennial in zones south of 8, but must be treated as an annual in the north.

Globe amaranth (Gomphrena) usually blooms in red purple or white. This particular one, which I found in a line of otherwise conventional colors, is pinkish—a color I have not seen before. Maybe it was a sport. Gomphrena likes it hot and dry, and is an annual. It is also very easy to dry.

How to Add Fragrance to the Garden

How to Add Fragrance to the Garden

The glorious fragrance of blooming plants is one of the greatest (and sometimes overlooked) joys a garden can give. To get a jump on the season and soften the winter chill, grow sweet-smelling paper-white narcissuses indoors and make a supply of potpourri in summer for the colder months ahead.

The following is a list of plants that will add a lovely scent to the garden. Some of them are discussed in other parts of the book.

WITCH HAZEL *(Hamamelis)*. These bloom in mid-February in my zone. A very tough plant with fringy sweet flowers. Try 'Arnold Promise,' for both its odor and nice autumn foliage. Zones 5–8.

MAGNOLIA STELLATA. Blooms in April. A small tree (25 feet) with lovely gray bark and an interesting shape. Zones 3–8.

WINTER HONEYSUCKLE *(Lonicera fragrantissima)*. Blooms in April and is easy to force in the house. Not much to look at, so should be planted where you can smell it but not have to depend on its adding much to the shape of the garden. (Behind the garage?) Zones 4–9.

HYACINTHS. All are fragrant. I like the single "wild" varieties. Zones 4–8.

NARCISSUS. Also all fragrant. Some more so than others, but as a group they throw out a powerful scent. Zones 4–8.

VIBURNUM JUDDII. An "improved" strain of the marvelous April-blooming favorite *V. carlesii*. Plant this small-scale shrub under a bedroom window. Zones 4–8.

Overleaf: *Fragrant lily*

LILAC (*Syringa*). Traditional fragrant shrub. 'Ellen Willmott' is white and 'Miss Kim' is delicate lavender, blooming later than the others. Both are fine performers. Zones 3–8.

RUSSIAN OLIVE (*Elaeagnus angustifolia*). Blooms in June and is hardy at the seashore. Should be carefully pruned to improve its shape, but is easy to grow. Zones 2–8.

ROSES. This is a very large and fairly familiar subject. Generally, the older, unhybridized plants are the most rewarding from a fragrance standpoint (and often visually as well). If you have limited space, try miniatures. 'Pacesetter,' which is white, and 'Starina,' which is scarlet, are both big award winners. Zones 5–10.

WISTERIA. This familiar vine has a lovely odor, but don't fool around with it unless you intend to keep it under control. It can really do damage otherwise. Zones 4–9.

CAROLINA JASMINE (*Gelsemium*). The climbing variety has an intoxicating scent, but likes a warm climate. However, it can be grown here with a warm wall in back of it and some winter protection. Zones 7–10.

SWEET AUTUMN CLEMATIS (*C. paniculata*), HONEYSUCKLE. These are two other climbers. Both need to be kept under control, but are not as destructive as wisteria. Zones 5–9.

LILY-OF-THE-VALLEY, SWEET WOODRUFF. Both of these provide fragrant ground cover and bloom from mid-May into June. Lily is hardy in Zones 3–9. Woodruff is hardy in Zones 4–8.

PINKS, CARNATIONS, SWEET WILLIAMS. This wonderfully fragrant family of plants make a nice splash of color in the garden, in addition to their scent. However, they run out of gas after several seasons and should be replaced. Zones 3–8.

LAVENDER. Everyone is familiar with the odor of lavender. These come in varying heights, but all have beautiful silvery foliage. 'Hidcote' is a good one about 18 inches tall, and a shorter strain, 'Munstead,' is about 12 inches tall. Zones 5–9.

LILIES. The July and August fragrance gap is filled by these splendid flowers, almost all of which are scented to some degree. Many are extremely fragrant. Buy them according to height and time of bloom. They are especially easy plants, just requiring good drainage. Zones 3–8.

HERBS. These are a special category. They usually have limited ornamental appeal but can certainly perfume the air. I don't use basil to cook with much anymore, but always put a dozen plants in the bed outside the dining-room window. Their odor is delightful. Don't overlook lemon balm, sage, rosemary, and thyme. I also have mint growing on a bank (it tends to spread very rapidly, so beware). When you walk through it in the tall grass, you get a great whiff of spearmint.

There are other plants, of course; this is just to get you started.

Mail-Order Seed Catalogs

There are many, many seed catalogs,
but here are my favorites.

W. ATLEE BURPEE CO.
300 Park Avenue at 18th Street
Warminster, Pennsylvania 18974

COOLEYS GARDEN
P.O. Box 126
Silverton, Oregon 97381

GEORGE W. PARK SEED CO., INC.
P.O. Box 31
Greenwood, South Carolina 29647

ROSES OF YESTERDAY AND TODAY
802 Brown's Valley Road
Watsonville, California 95076

JOHN SCHEEPERS, INC.
63 Wall Street
New York, New York 10005

THOMPSON & MORGAN
P.O. Box 100
Farmingdale, New Jersey 07727

K. VAN BOURGONDIEN & SONS, INC.
Box A, 245 Farmingdale Road
Babylon, New York 11702

THE WAYSIDE GARDENS COMPANY
Hodges, South Carolina 29695

WHITE FLOWER FARM
Litchfield, Connecticut 06759

GILBERT H. WILD & SON, INC.
Sarcoxie, Missouri 64862

Index

Page numbers in *italics* refer to
  illustrations.